UNDERSTANDING
JULIAN BARNES

Understanding Contemporary British Literature
Matthew J. Bruccoli, General Editor

Understanding Kingsley Amis
by Merritt Moseley
Understanding Martin Amis
by James Diedrick
Understanding Julian Barnes
by Merritt Mosely
Understanding John Fowles
by Thomas C. Foster
Understanding Graham Greene
by R. H. Miller
Understanding Doris Lessing
by Jean Pickering
Understanding Iris Murdoch
by Cheryl K. Bove
Understanding Harold Pinter
by Ronald Knowles
Understanding Arnold Wesker
by Robert Wilcher
Understanding Paul West
by David W. Madden

UNDERSTANDING
Julian
BARNES

by Merritt Moseley

THE UNIVERSITY OF SOUTH CAROLINA PRESS

Cloth edition published by the University of South Carolina Press, 1997
Paperback edition published in Columbia, South Carolina,
by the University of South Carolina Press, 2009

www.sc.edu/uscpress

Manufactured in the United States of America

18 17 16 15 14 13 12 11 10 09   10 9 8 7 6 5 4 3 2 1

The Library of Congress has cataloged the cloth edition as follows:
Moseley, Merritt, 1949–
    Understanding Julian Barnes / by Merritt Moseley.
        p. cm. — (Understanding contemporary British literature)
    Includes bibliographical references and index.
    ISBN 1-57003-140-1
    1. Barnes, Julian—Criticism and interpretation. I. Title. II. Series.
    PR6052.A6657Z76   1997
    823'.914—dc20   96—25197

ISBN: 978-1-57003-875-4 (pbk)

For my daughters,
Eleanor, Mary, Claire, and Elizabeth,
with love

CONTENTS

Editor's Preface   ix

Acknowledgments   x

Chapter 1 Career and Overview   1

Chapter 2 *Metroland*   18

Chapter 3 Duffy   33

Chapter 4 *Before She Met Me*   54

Chapter 5 *Flaubert's Parrot*   69

Chapter 6 *Staring at the Sun*   91

Chapter 7 *A History of the World in 10½ Chapters*   108

Chapter 8 *Talking It Over*   125

Chapter 9 *The Porcupine*   145

Chapter 10 Short Stories and Nonfiction   158

Chapter 11 Conclusion   170

Notes   173

Bibliography   188

Index   195

EDITOR'S PREFACE

The volumes of *Understanding Contemporary British Literature* have been planned as guides or companions for students as well as good nonacademic readers. The editor and publisher perceive a need for these volumes because much of the influential contemporary literature makes special demands. Uninitiated readers encounter difficulty in approaching works that depart from the traditional forms and techniques of prose and poetry. Literature relies on conventions, but the conventions keep evolving; new writers form their own conventions—which in time may become familiar. Put simply, *UCBL* provides instruction in how to read certain contemporary writers—identifying and explicating their material, themes, use of language, point of view, structures, symbolism, and responses to experience.

The word *understanding* in the titles was deliberately chosen. Many willing readers lack an adequate understanding of how contemporary literature works; that is, what the author is attempting to express and the means by which it is conveyed. Although the criticism and analysis in the series have been aimed at a level of general accessibility, these introductory volumes are meant to be applied in conjunction with the works they cover. They do not provide a substitute for the works and authors they introduce, but rather prepare the reader for more profitable literary experiences.

M. J. B.

ACKNOWLEDGMENTS

In writing this book I have received generous support and encouragement from Matthew Bruccoli and the staff of the University of South Carolina Press; from my colleagues in the Department of Literature at the University of North Carolina at Asheville and those at University College, Chester; and from the librarians at UNCA's Ramsey Library. Among individuals, I have profited most from conversations with Glyn Turton and Michael Gillum.

As always I have enjoyed the support and understanding of my family. My thanks to my wife Madeline and to my daughters, to whom this book is dedicated.

UNDERSTANDING
JULIAN BARNES

CHAPTER ONE

Career and Overview

Career

Since beginning his career as a novelist in 1980, Julian Barnes has been called "the chameleon of British letters"; a writer "like the teacher of your dreams: joky, metaphorical across both popular and unpopular culture, epigrammatic"; and, less admiringly, "a brilliant essayist whom fashion and financial logic directed towards the novel."[1] He is the author of seven novels published under his own name, four detective thrillers published under the name Dan Kavanagh, and a considerable amount of periodical short fiction and miscellaneous nonfiction.

In his fiction he has pursued two divergent paths: in the four Dan Kavanagh, or Duffy (the name of his detective), books, he has not only practiced genre fiction but done so in a formulaic or repetitive way—that is, written a series of books with the same major character and same general plot structure. Meanwhile, in his career as author of "mainstream" novels, his books have resisted categorization and defied expectations to a remarkable degree.[2] Each one is markedly different from the ones which have preceded it. Barnes's admiration for Gustave Flaubert is clear from the way he writes about him, especially in his fourth novel, *Flaubert's Parrot;* and he admires him most of all because Flaubert is "a great example of a genius who never wrote the same book twice."[3] Though he might not nominate himself as a genius, he would undoubtedly be pleased to be seen as that same kind of writer. The American writer Jay McInerny, one of his friends, believes he is:

> A lot of novelists set up a kind of franchise, and turn out a familiar product. . . . what I like about Jules's work is that he's like an entrepreneur who starts up a new company every time out. . . . He reinvents the wheel; I'm always fascinated to see what shape it's going to be next.[4]

The future chameleon was born in Leicester, in England's East Midlands, on 19 January 1946. His parents were teachers of French; perhaps Barnes's long and productive interest in France and French literature began with them. Though he writes often and thoughtfully about religious belief, his upbringing was without religion ("I've never been to a church service," he commented in 1989).[5] In 1956 the family moved to Northwood, in the northwestern suburbs of London; this area of Middlesex, served by London Underground's Metropolitan line, provided the title for and the early setting of Barnes's first novel, *Metroland* (1980). Barnes's attitude toward the suburban milieu of his youth is oddly ambivalent; asked by Mira Stout in 1992 whether he liked the place where he spent his youth, he not only sounds ambivalent but almost seems never to have considered the question before: "Well, I *quite* liked it at the time. I mean, I didn't *hate* it I don't think. . . . Yeah, maybe I did. . . . Yeah, I did in fact. Yeah, I did actually. I *did* hate it. That's true; I *loathed* it."[6] Barnes commuted by rail from Northwood to the City of London School from 1957 to 1964, where he was an "uncompetitive" student

CAREER AND OVERVIEW

who joined the stamp club; from there he went on to Magdalen College, Oxford, which he says was not "a recipe for either happiness or achievement" and where he read modern languages and took his B.A. (Honours) in 1968. In 1966–67 he spent the academic year as an English teacher at a Catholic school in Rennes, France.[7]

There followed a period spent in semiacademic work, preparation for a career in the law which never materialized, and freelance writing. In 1969 he joined the staff of the *Oxford English Dictionary,* where he stayed for three years. He has explained that, as a male among a female majority, he was given most of the "rude words and sports words" to handle.[8] His connoisseurship in language can only have been sharpened by this experience.

While working on the *OED,* Barnes met the poet Craig Raine, who introduced him to the novelist Martin Amis, at that time an editor at the *Times Literary Supplement.* Barnes began reviewing books for the *TLS* in 1973; in 1977 he became deputy literary editor of the *New Statesman,* also under Amis. Though he studied law (1972–74) and actually qualified as a barrister, he has never practiced, explaining: "I took all the exams, but I was getting more pleasure out of doing a round-up of four novels for a provincial paper than I was out of preparing what I might say defending some criminal."[9] In 1975 he began a column on the *New Review,* using the pseudonym Edward Pygge; he has also been television critic of *The Observer* and written a restaurant column for the *Tatler,* using as his pseudonym "Basil Seal," the name of one of Evelyn Waugh's characters. One account of his busy freelance writing career says that he "resigned from all of it on his 40th birthday."[10] This is not quite true, as he still writes reviews for various journals, including *The New York Review of Books,* and has been *The New Yorker*'s London correspondent since 1990, writing about politics, mostly, but also such matters as the *fatwa* against Salman Rushdie, the comic misadventures of Chancellor Norman Lamont, the Royal Family, and garden mazes. Suspicious about the wisdom of reprinting reviews, Barnes has not collected his copious nonfiction written for English journals or his reviews, in book form, though his *Letters from London* for *The New Yorker* were collected and published in 1995.[11]

Nevertheless, the balance of his output between nonfiction of various kinds and book-length fiction certainly changed dramatically in 1980, when his first two books were published. One of them, *Metroland,* is a long-gestated coming-of-age novel about a young man growing up in the same suburbs as Barnes, with the same interest in French matters, the same loathing for bourgeois conformity. Written in three parts, it gives an account of Christopher Lloyd's early adolescence; his somewhat later adolescence, including a sexual initiation, in Paris in 1968; and his married and working life back in London. Commenting on the timing of *Metroland,* the novelist explains:

> *Metroland* took me seven to eight years from start to finish. Now I look at it and think it was an 18-month book, but I was very lacking in confidence. I took a long time convincing myself that I had anything to say or that I was capable of writing a novel and so it sat in a drawer for a year at a time and went through a lot of re-writing.[12]

The novel was well received, even if not uniformly so. It received the 1981 Somerset Maugham award, given to an outstanding first novel.

In the same year as *Metroland,* but under the name Dan Kavanagh, he published his first detective thriller, *Duffy.* The parallel tracks on which he continued publishing mainstream, "literary" novels, every other year or so, under his own name while publishing four Kavanagh books in six years constitute a peculiar feature of the author's output. Julian Barnes never writes the same book twice. Dan Kavanagh, arguably, writes the same book four times. The use of a bisexual, ambiguously disgraced former policeman as his detective is unusual, but otherwise the detective books are not experimental in any way, making a marked contrast to the innovation and frequently postmodern *jouissance* of their better-known, and openly acknowledged, siblings.

Barnes has given various explanations of this part of his career, the most straightforward being that he liked to read thrillers and decided to write them, using a pseudonym for them to avoid confusion in his public perception.[13] The fact that he writes the detective books in a different place (borrowing detective novelist Ruth Rendell's cottage, for instance) and even on a different typewriter and prefers not to answer questions about them when he is in his own home (that is, the place where he writes the Julian Barnes books) makes the divided career a bit more intriguing. One might hypothesize that the traditionalist side of Julian Barnes, the part of him that appreciates straightforward narration, the management of suspense, and a fairly clear moral taxonomy among the characters, has gone into the making of the Duffy books, leaving him free in his other novels to experiment, to rearrange or dispense with narrative chronology, to be playful about the relationship between art and life.

Duffy was followed by *Fiddle City* in 1981, *Putting the Boot In* in 1985, and *Going to the Dogs* in 1987. Barnes is scrupulous about researching the factual bases for his books, and each is set in a strongly marked and interesting London subculture: respectively, the Soho sex industry, Heathrow Airport, a lower-division football club, and (though less centrally) the world of dog racing and petty villainy. He has tired of using a recyclable hero, and the Duffy books seem to have stopped.

Following *Metroland* Barnes has published a "regular" novel roughly every two years. *Before She Met Me* (1982) is a short but intense, funny but terrifying study of love and over-mastering jealousy. Published in 1984, *Flaubert's Parrot* was Barnes's first great success; as he remarks, "it's the book that launched me."[14] It was also the first of his books to raise the question (a recurrent one in reviews of Barnes's works) of whether it deserves to be called a novel at all. This question may have been given added point when *Flaubert's Parrot* won the 1986 Prix Médicis, a French award (never before given to an Englishman) more often awarded for a book of essays.

In 1986 *Staring at the Sun* appeared to subdued acclaim. In part the disappointed reaction of many readers may be explained by the perception that after *Flaubert's Parrot* this is a step back into a quieter mainstream, with a main character, Jean Sergeant, who is too ordinary for some tastes. Barnes is eloquent in defending this book against the tone of reviews, which he thinks (among the British at least) tend to be "unadventurous."[15]

CAREER AND OVERVIEW

A History of the World in 10½ Chapters (1989) has been his other nearly unanimous critical success. Like *Flaubert's Parrot,* it takes liberties with the novel form and invites suspicion over whether it qualifies as a novel at all. An ambitious book, it is a collection of ten chapters, not all of which are narratives (one is an essay in art criticism, for instance), roughly chronological— the first chapter is about Noah's ark; the last, about the afterlife— and dedicated to the exploration of serious themes in a serious way, while remaining witty and often charming. The half chapter is a (perhaps) straightforward disquisition on love.

After *A History* came *Talking It Over* (1991), which is like *Before She Met Me* in being a contemporary study of relations between men and women, set in London, but has a very different tone and technique. *The Porcupine* (1992) is yet another departure, this time into a specifically political fiction set in a fictionalized former Communist country, much like Bulgaria, and invoking the moral complexities of freedom, truth, and political power. In 1996 he published his first book of short fiction. Called *Cross Channel,* it collects ten stories on the subject of historical and cultural encounters between the English and France.

In 1979 Barnes married Pat Kavanagh, a well-known literary agent, to whom six of his novels are dedicated. That the first of these is *Duffy,* the author of which is identified as Dan Kavanagh, suggests the origin of that pseudonym. The couple is childless.

In England there has been a controversy over the fact that Barnes has never won the Booker Prize, the most prestigious award for a novel written by an author from Britain, Ireland, or the Commonwealth. In 1984 *Flaubert's Parrot* made the short list (was one of the six finalists); *A History of the World in 10½ Chapters,* his other most highly praised novel, did not even make the short list. Controversy is what keeps interest in the Booker Prize alive, of course, and a look at some of the winners suggests that it is by no means an infallible guide to the best book of any given year. Aside from the Booker, Barnes has been rewarded by many prizes; in addition to the Somerset Maugham award and the Prix Médicis, he has received the Geoffrey Faber Memorial Prize (1985); the E. M. Forster Award (1986); an American Academy and Institute of Arts and Letters award (1986); a Gutenberg prize (French; 1987); the Prix Femina (1992) for *Love, Etc.,* the French translation of *Talking It Over*; and the Shakespeare Prize from the FVS Foundation of Hamburg (1993). In 1988 he was made a Chevalier de l'Ordre des Arts et des Lettres.

Overview

The quality of Julian Barnes's fiction that attracts the most comment is its technique. Sometimes, particularly in reference to *Flaubert's Parrot* and *A History of the World in 10½ Chapters,* the comment has amounted to challenging these books' right to be called novels at all. Some detractors imply that he is an essayist who finds it easier to be published and read by pretending that his essays are really chapters in novels. David Sexton summarizes this line of thought as follows:

> Barnes writes books which look like novels and get shelved as novels but which, when you open them up, are some-

thing else altogether. *Flaubert's Parrot* was for the most part a set of studies of Flaubert and his parrot. His new book, *A History of the World in 10½ Chapters,* is even odder. The 10 chapters contain 10 quite different stories, some factual, some not. They are related only by image and theme.[16]

To this there are several responses.[17] One is that the generalization is built on only two of Barnes's seven, or eleven counting the Duffy titles, novels. Another is that the rather querulous challenge to Barnes's novels is based on an implied claim that is itself untrue: that some universal consensus exists on what a novel is. Many books far more unusual than Julian Barnes's are accepted as novels. It seems that only critics in England, where modernist experimentation has been viewed with a good deal more suspicion than in the United States, fret about whether or not these are novels. Barnes's own definition of the novel, designed to include *A History,* is not an unacceptable one: "It's an extended piece of prose, largely fictional, which is planned and executed as a whole piece."[18] In conversation with Mark Lawson, he responded to the same kind of complaint (also about *A History*): "My line now is I'm a novelist and if I say it's a novel, it is. . . . And it's not terribly interesting to me, casting people out of the realm of fiction. Okay, let's throw out Rabelais, Diderot and Kundera. . . ."[19]

The characteristics with which some reviewers take issue in the two most untraditional novels are, first, a principle of construction different from chronological narration—more broadly, a higher than usual percentage of something other than narration entirely, such as a Flaubert chronology and a Flaubert bestiary, a chapter of art criticism and an essay on love in *A History*—and, second, a high degree of intelligence, of learning, of philosophical investigation. *Flaubert's Parrot* is quite a reliable introduction to the life and works of the French author in which Barnes's own well-attested love for his works shines through the thoughts of his duller narrator, Geoffrey Braithwaite; *A History* is based on thoroughly mastered information about Mt. Ararat, medieval church trials, and many other topics (*related* topics, despite their surface miscellaneity); and both deal ambitiously with important questions such as the relationship between art and life, or the nature of history, or the meaning of love.

To believe that such features mean that a book is not a novel is to have too narrow a view of the novel. Barnes's own fullest statement on the subject deserves to be the final one:

> I don't take too much notice of the "but-does-he-write-proper-novels?" school of criticism, which I get a bit, especially in England. . . . I feel closer to the continental idea—which used to be the English idea as well—that the novel is a very broad and generous enclosing form. I would argue for greater inclusivity rather than any exclusivity. The novel always starts with life, always has to start with life rather than an intellectual grid which you then impose on things. But at the same time, formally and structurally, I don't see why it shouldn't be inventive and playful and break what supposed rules there are.[20]

Looking over the whole prospect of Barnes's mainstream novels, it is possible to characterize his technical concerns more broadly. One is his determination to challenge himself and the limits of the genre. Described by Mira Stout as something of a "challenge addict," he has explained his own reasons for always making it new: "In order to write, you have to convince yourself that it's a new departure for you and not only a new departure for you but for the entire history of the novel."[21] Such a conviction might be thought of as daunting; but despite his usual modesty in talking about his books, Barnes is obviously daring. And he insists that his books can be risk-taking in more ways than the obvious deviation from conventional structure—that, in short, *Flaubert's Parrot* and *A History of the World in 10½ Chapters* are not his only daring books, punctuated by safe and ordinary novels in between. He made his detective Duffy bisexual because he thought it had not been done before and would clearly represent a challenge. About his *Staring at the Sun*, he thinks it "is slightly underrated, in that it looks less adventurous than *Flaubert's Parrot*, but I think it took a fair amount of risks. . . ."[22]

The constants in Barnes's oeuvre, aside from change, include a dedication to accuracy and elegance of language, and perfection of rhythm and lucidity. He likes to quote Flaubert's dictum: "Prose is like hair. It shines with combing."[23] He is witty. His books are, for the most part, funny, though they are not necessarily comedies. The two funniest books may be the ones that have the least-comic plot trajectories, *Before She Met Me* and *Talking It Over*. The comedy is in the language and the texture, not the events of the plots. Barnes has a wit that accompanies his relish for words. His wit is also found in striking and original figurative language. Often a character who is by no stretch of the imagination an authorial representative—for instance the unbalanced rake Oliver in *Talking It Over*—operates with a rich, fluent, and funny linguistic gift.

Barnes is as artistically aware of structure as he is of texture. The concern for construction has been evident from *Metroland* on. That novel's three sections, each dramatizing a short but significant period of the protagonist's life, are carefully shaped for both parallelism and significant contrast—the parallelism giving point to the contrast. In larger works Barnes may choose to set thematically grounded constructions off against apparent randomness, or at least looseness, of form. This is most noticeable in *A History of the World in 10½ Chapters*. The looseness is no illusion; but there are principles of construction that artfully link the apparently discordant and heterogeneous parts.

As his insistence that the novel starts with life, rather than an intellectual grid, implies, Barnes is no empty technician. Probably he would not agree with the Flaubert who wanted to write a book with no content, consisting only of style. David Coward, reviewing *Flaubert's Parrot,* wrote penetratingly that "The modern British novel finds it easy to be clever and comic. Barnes also manages that much harder thing: he succeeds in communicating genuine emotion without affectation or embarrassment."[24] Barnes's persistent concern—more than previous works of literature, more than experimentation with form, more than "the modern condition"—is love. Each of his novels is about love in some central if not exclusive way. It is indirect and oblique in *Flaubert's Parrot,* disturbed and painful in *Before She Met Me,* evanescent in *Staring at the Sun,* complicated by ambition and duty in *The Porcupine,* but it is there always. On the relationship between men and women, including marriage, unhappy and frustrated longings, and particularly sexual jealousy, he has written compellingly. Speaking about *Before She Met Me,* he delivers a judgment that applies more widely to all his books: "what is constant is the human heart and human passions."[25] It is no sentimentalization; the ways in which love makes men and women unhappy are expertly traced in several of his novels. But in his most ambitious treatment of the importance of love, he declares that even though it may not make people happy, it is what will save them from the forces of history.

Perhaps surprisingly, Barnes's focus is usually on married, even though sometimes marred, love. *Before She Met Me, Metroland,* and *Talking It Over* are, broadly speaking, studies of marriage; so, though in a considerably more oblique way, are *Flaubert's Parrot* and *Staring at the Sun.* His most political novel, *The Porcupine,* reveals the effect on a marriage of political commitment and ethical compromise. Even his most ambitious and compendious novel, *A History of the World in 10½ Chapters,* devotes a considerable amount of its attention to marriage. And in the "half" chapter, a meditation on love, Julian Barnes claims to speak in his own name, as Julian Barnes; thus, his claims about love, and his description of his own relations with his beloved, may plausibly be assigned to his own marriage, and his beloved may plausibly be identified as his wife, Pat Kavanagh, to whom the book is dedicated.

Crucially connected with this interest in marriage is the subject of infidelity and adultery, or cuckoldry. Barnes's male protagonists are often the "victims" of their wives' infidelity, though his subtlety in his approach makes "victim" seem far too crude a concept. In a survey of the role of cuckolds in Western literature, Mark I. Millington and Alison S. Sinclair assert that

> there are two models or paradigms for the portrayal of the offended husband: either he is mocked for the situation he finds himself in, or he is admired for his attitude and action in the face of his wife's infidelity. That is, he is portrayed either as a cuckold or as a man of honour.[26]

This formulation is meant to apply primarily to literature of the medieval and Renaissance periods. The authors go on to assert that the cuckold is a stock figure of mirth and ridicule, while the man of honor (whom they identify as embodying Melanie Klein's "paranoid-schizoid position"[27]) is an inflexible, self-righteous figure of vengeance whose retaliation for his mistreatment upholds the patriarchal system.

But Julian Barnes's cuckolds fit these categories hardly at all (as Millington and Sinclair acknowledge when they identify *Before She Met Me* as a "mixing of elements from the two models").[28] The avengers among Barnes's cuckolds—chiefly Graham in *Before She Met Me* but in a less spectacular way Stuart in *Talking It Over*—are not in fact cuckolds. While Stuart's wife has fallen in love with another man and thus betrayed Stuart, she is not having an affair. And Graham's wife is perfectly faithful to him; her only fault lies in having had an active sex life in her past, which becomes Graham's present-day obsession.

On the other hand Barnes gives his readers models of men whose wives actually have been unfaithful to them—most nota-

CAREER AND OVERVIEW

bly Chris in *Metroland* and Geoffrey Braithwaite in *Flaubert's Parrot*—and shows that they are not comic, as conventional cuckolds are supposed to be—at least in part because there is no suggestion that either of them has brought his cuckoldry on himself by "lack of potency . . . foolishness, gullibility, failure to be aware of what goes on."[29] Life, like Julian Barnes's fiction, is much more complex than the stock comic portrayals of laughable cuckolds require. And neither Chris nor Geoffrey retaliates in any way, except under the theory, acknowledged as a suspicion though denied, even by Braithwaite himself, that Geoffrey killed his wife. His reaction to his wife's vagaries is a sort of wistful equanimity; Chris expresses a somewhat hurt hopefulness. Both (like Leopold Bloom in James Joyce's *Ulysses*) react to the threat of replacement not by slaughtering their wives or their rivals or both—a kind of behavior that appears in Barnes's fiction not as the satisfaction of honor but as derangement—but by mental adjustment.

Millington and Sinclair's history shows that the stock cuckold has not only lost his exclusive rights to his wife through his own fault, but by failing to do anything about his loss (failure to act as a man of honor) forfeits his right to the reader's sympathy, deservedly becoming an object of contemptuous amusement. Barnes's real cuckolds react more thoughtfully and pacifically than those who are technically not cuckolded or are only mentally cuckolded (for example, in the mind of the husband), but without becoming foolish or contemptible.

A devotion to the centrality of human passions may strike a somewhat surprising note for a man sometimes caricatured as a thoroughgoing postmodernist with all the skepticism about values and the possibility of knowledge that that position usually entails; so does his literary credo, delivered to Patrick McGrath, which sounds more like George Eliot than Samuel Beckett:

> I think I'm a moralist. . . . Part of a novelist's job obviously is to understand as wide a variety of people as possible. And you put them in situations where there isn't necessarily an easy answer, and things aren't necessarily resolved. But this doesn't mean you don't have strong personal views about how life should be lived, and what's good and bad behavior, as I certainly do.[30]

There are other recurrent subjects in Barnes's fiction, perhaps most insistently France and the English in contact with that nearby but ultimately very different culture. A final important common element in Barnes's work is a sustained interest in serious ideas and a willingness to engage them in his fictions. To call a work "a novel of ideas" is sometimes to imply a deadening book, a disguised treatise, a forum for disembodied figures little more than authorial puppets to exchange the author's thoughts with each other for the reader's benefit. Julian Barnes never writes a book answering this description, yet he does write novels of ideas. As a modern liberal thinker, aware of complexity, he writes books richer in the exploration of serious ideas than in the delivery of finality and doctrinaire answers. *The Porcupine* not only examines the competing claims of freedom and control but is a subtle investigation of the perennial question of whether or to what extent ends can justify means. *Flaubert's Parrot* and *A History of the World in 10½ Chapters* raise the question—among

CAREER AND OVERVIEW

the most important questions human beings face—of whether they can know the truth. *Staring at the Sun* asks why they go on living and whether there is a god. One does not read his books to discover what the right answers are about, say, the relationship between the author's life and the work, or history's reliability; and when he does seem to speak in his own voice, as occasionally in *History,* his "truths" are contingent and hesitant.

Nevertheless they are there. And this is another reason why Julian Barnes is one of the most interesting, challenging figures now writing in English. Under the age of fifty, and having published his first novel at thirty-four, he has already produced a distinguished body of work. His daring, his challenge to himself to make every book a new departure not only for Julian Barnes but for the whole history of the novel, makes each of his books an event. And his unique mixture of literary experimentation, intelligence, and dedication to the truths of the human heart—what has been called "an extraordinarily artful mix of literary tomfoolery and high seriousness"—makes every book an adventure.[31]

CHAPTER TWO

Metroland

A first novel is the book in an author's career most likely to be autobiographical. If a novelist is to write a coming-of-age book, it is probably going to be the first book. Julian Barnes is no exception. *Metroland* contains more autobiography than any of his other novels; though the central events are not necessarily taken from his life, many of the details of setting and character certainly are. Like *A Portrait of the Artist as a Young Man* or *The Red and the Black,* it is the story of a bright and witty young man, at odds with his environment and rebelling through art, and his coming to maturity. That this maturing process involves a shrinking of horizons and an acceptance of the ordinary is part of the realism of this book.

Looking back on *Metroland* from the vantage of Barnes's later novels, it is possible to see how it announces concerns that will be repeated. There is, for instance, France, as both a place and a psychological influence on the English. The protagonist not only goes to France in 1968 but even earlier, as an ordinary teenager living in Metroland, habitually uses French culture as an index of the shortcomings of suburban London. He is conversant with *symboliste* poetry, lines from which turn up in the novel as epigraphs; he and his best friend adopt as their project to *écraser l'infame* and *épater la bourgeoisie* (crush the infamous thing—Voltaire's motto—and shock the bourgeois), scoring "epats" by moderately outrageous behavior; he tries to take the curse off his suburban Eastwick home by saying in French, "j'habite Metroland."[1]

METROLAND

This novel is a triptych, written in three parts called "Metroland (1963)," "Paris (1968)," and "Metroland II (1977)." The tripartite structure seems particularly congenial to Barnes, as well as particularly shapely, and will recur in *Staring at the Sun* and *Talking It Over*. Here the three sections are of unequal dimensions, the first being almost as long as the other two combined. There is considerable structural similarity among the three parts. Each begins with a one-or two-page scene-setting introduction followed by a series of short chapters, all titled with evocative and sometimes ironic phrases such as "The Constructive Loaf" or "J'habite Metroland" or "Nude, Giant Girls." In each of the three parts the last chapter is called "Object Relations" and addresses the objects that mark this stage of the protagonist's development.

The tone of the novel is assured and charming. Always acute about language, Barnes depicts a protagonist who is himself precociously verbal. Though Christopher is sixteen in the first section, the voice of the narrator is older. Presumably the narrative perspective is that of the thirty-year-old Christopher of part 3, who is now capable of ironic correction of the ideas and postures of his adolescent self. The first-person narration combines an inhabiting of the mind of the adolescent with an older man's understanding of that mind's shortcomings.

In part 1 Barnes creates a telling, detailed, and amusing picture of youth. He deftly accomplishes what must be a difficult aim: to make this picture both representative and individual, an account of both adolescence and an adolescent. Among Christopher Lloyd's preoccupations are many that are, if not universal, still common to young men. He is obsessed with sex, though without any practical knowledge of it. He is offended by his parents, brother, and sister and, in an illustration of the "family romance" that Freud claimed as a common fantasy, suspects that the commonplace people represented to him as his family must be some sort of impostors:

> Could it be that I was really related to all of them? And how could I bear not to point out the obvious differences?
> "Mum, am I illegitimate?"
> . . . .
> "You sure there isn't a chance I'm illegitimate?" I waved an explicatory hand towards [siblings] Nigel and Mary. (40)

He takes genuine delight in being called "sir" and treasures the first time it happened, which was also when he was being measured for his first pair of long trousers. He feels contempt for almost all his contemporaries and all the older people he knows, especially those in positions of authority in his school, reserving his respect for older people he does not know, like Albert Camus.

All these are, one might say, generic traits of adolescence, though they are captured in original ways in Barnes's narration. A perhaps more unusual trait, and one that is more lasting for Christopher, is fear of death. This is not a fear of dying but of being dead: he explains, "I wouldn't mind Dying at all, I thought, as long as I didn't end up Dead at the end of it" (54). This dread dates from about the same time that he lost his belief in God. Though it is unclear that loss of God produced fear of death, he does acknowledge that one of his religion substitutes, art, produced some consolation for his death fears. It is inadequate, and it is not until he is a married man that he finally, somewhat to his own surprise, discovers that he is no longer troubled by "big D" (53).

The other ways in which Christopher Lloyd is made an original and individual adolescent have to do with his friend Toni. In an unsympathetic review, Paul Bailey comments: "Novels written in the first person, novels intent on establishing the peculiar quality of a single life, survive when they set that life against a vivid background of other, possibly more interesting lives. There is a curious lack of people in *Metroland*."[2] The generalization in the first sentence is debatable, of course; the observation in the second has some force. To the young Christopher, most people are fools or stooges or ridiculous bourgeois or possible targets of an "epat" or an "ecras." They do not fully exist. The "lack of people" is not a sign of careless writing but apt characterization of a self-absorbed adolescent, impatient of other people because his categories are so selective and literary that hardly anybody *can* exist for him.

And the fact is that at least one person is fully present and very important, both to Christopher and in the economy of the novel, that is, to the reader: his friend Toni. The companion of most of his leisure time, spent in observing people at the museum, in feigning French culture, in laughing at the rugby team, in dreaming about their future (Toni's vision is that they will be "artists-in-residence at a nudist colony" [70]), Toni is the most important secondary character in *Metroland*—clearly in part 1, where he is the one who shares Christopher's life and ideas; less clearly in part 2, where he is only an absent inspiration and monitor; and crucially in part 3, where he judges Christopher the grownup harshly for not having fulfilled his youthful ambitions.

It is in creating the imaginative lives of Christopher and Toni that Barnes produces the strongly individual character of the adolescent scenes. Toni shares the admiration for French culture, made up in roughly equal parts of (1) longing for something different from their normal English milieu; (2) attraction to the idea of the "sophisticated tough" as represented by Henry de Montherlant and Albert Camus; (3) desire to be *flaneurs* (sophisticated urban idlers or boulevardiers)—Christopher and Toni try being flaneurs but are handicapped by the lack of a boulevard; and (4) snobbery. Sometimes the snobbery takes the form of using their own superiority in the French language to get away with substituting "syphilisée" for "civilizée" in French conversation class.[3]

French language and culture are also associated for them with sex and, even more, with art, which they agree is "the most important thing in life, the constant to which one could be unfailingly devoted and which would never cease to reward . . ." (29). Their way of experiencing art, aside from writing in journals, is to visit museums in a therapeutic way; any visit to any museum, since it includes ingesting art, is seen as valuable. There is something more than a little philistine, by the way, in Christopher's and Toni's museum visits; though they go there to mock philistines, they assume that art is good for them, hardly the tough modernist stance of their heroes.

As well as looking at the paintings, Toni and Christopher like to look at other people, primarily to sneer. It is in sneering, actually, that their own youthful rebellion largely consists, and French seems to help them, providing a stance and a language for sneering. At what? Christopher provides a partial list: "dummos, prefects, masters, parents, my brother and sister, Third Division (North) football, Moliére, God, the bourgeoisie and normal people . . ." (37–38). These are the things they hate, along with elegiac oldsters met on the train; more "politically"—though in terms of any real political interest, perhaps aside from an interest in left-wing rebelliousness copied from Sartre, they are inert— there is a sort of rebelliousness against an unfocused "they": the "unidentified legislators, moralists, social luminaries and parents of outer suburbia" (14).

Part 1 presents Christopher's situation, along with that of Toni, through a series of short vignettes: Christopher on the train, going into London every day (like Julian Barnes) to his school; Christopher in reaction against an uncle; Christopher trying to impress his older brother's girlfriend, failing, then scoring her badly on the SST scale he and Toni use (SST stands for soul, suffering, and tits). It is self-consciously an evocation of adolescence. In the chapter called "Object Relations" the narrator philosophizes:

> How does adolescence come back most vividly to you? What do you remember first? The quality of your parents; a girl; your first sexual tremor; success or failure at school; some still unconfessed humiliation; happiness; unhappiness; or, perhaps, a trivial action which first revealed to you what you might later become? I remember things. (71)

This chapter consists of a look around his room with comments on its contents, as will the two chapters with the same title in parts 2 and 3. This roomful of props—Monet poster, books by Rimbaud and Baudelaire, a suitcase with imaginary labels for the travels yet ahead—"objects redolent of all I felt and hoped for" (72)—prepares for the next stage in Christopher's progress, Paris in 1968.

Christopher and Toni are attractive youths in part 1, as literary characters usually are when they are brighter and wittier than those about them, and readers see their wit, their barbed comments, and not those of the others. A scene like the one where they ridicule the losing rugby team with exaggeratedly enthusiastic cheering is very funny. At the same time, they are clearly more immature than they think they are, and it is possible to understand how obnoxious they must be to their families and others around them. This perception prepares the reader for part 3, in which Christopher has changed much more than Toni, who remains obnoxious in a way characteristic of their younger days; still, Toni somehow seems to be more "right" than Christopher, since he has remained "true" to their youthful ideas (and the behavioral style that accompanied them) while Christopher has somehow "betrayed" them.

The usually gentle irony with which the adult narrator treats the adolescent Christopher becomes even more appropriate in section 2. It begins with an explanation, couched in the form of a later conversation with a disbelieving interlocutor, of how he was in Paris in summer of 1968 but missed what everybody else wants to know about: "*les événements,*" the student uprisings that

METROLAND

nearly brought down the government. Insofar as he knew anything about it, he dismissed the troubles as unimportant; what
was important was his love life with his French lover Annick.
Having spent an adolescence building up an image of France as
the home of alienation and political toughness, Christopher
misses all the reality and substitutes a romantic life of nearly
complete domesticity.

The official purpose of going to Paris is to write a thesis,
which he has invented in order to get a grant to go there; the real
purpose is "to immerse myself in the culture, the language, the
street-life, and—I would doubtless have added, with hesitant
casualness—the women" (105; he has not moved very far from
soul, suffering, and tits). In all of these aims Christopher succeeds, but usually in some way more ordinary than he had
expected. When he is being most self-consciously "Parisian"—
trying hard to be a flaneur, writing a set of precious Baudelairean
prose poems called "Spleenters"—he is being least honest. When
he meets Annick in an espresso bar, where he is able to start a
conversation because she is reading a Lawrence Durrell book, he
begins to grow up. Not only does he sleep with her and lose his
long-preserved virginity (to the sardonic epistolary applause of
Toni back home), he learns something about honesty and authen-
ticity, as opposed to bookishness. Annick calmly points out to
him that he pretends to know things he does not know; she elicits
from him the admission that a sexual position they tried out at his
suggestion, painfully enough, was something he had read about
in a book. He even tells her the truth about his reaction to sleeping
with her the first time—"[s]mugness and gratitude" (100).

In a complex reflection on the lessons learned from Annick, the narrator explains:

> Until I met Annick I'd always been certain that the edgy cynicism and disbelief in which I dealt, plus a cowed trust in the word of any imaginative writer, were the only tools for the painful, wrenching extraction of truths from the surrounding quartz of hypocrisy and deceit. The pursuit of truth had always seemed something combative. Now, not exactly in a flash, but over a few weeks, I wondered if it weren't something both higher—above the supposed conflict—and simpler, attainable not through striving but a simple inward glance. (101)

The honesty is not absolute, however, and this novel's suggestion is that it can never really be absolute.

The other crucial element in Christopher's Parisian education occurs when he meets three young English people, two boys and a girl, in a museum; ever pretentious, he pretends to be French in order to expose and chide what seems to be their philistinism but in fact is an elaborate game (the one who pretends to be baffled by Odilon Redon is doing a thesis on him). Gradually he becomes friendly with them—gradually becomes even more friendly with the girl, Marion, than with Mickey and Dave. Finally his guilty, but not quite candid, admission to Annick of how much time he has been spending with Marion leads Annick to leave him for good. The grounds are still dishonesty; she interprets his fumbling attempts to bring her up-to-date on his "amie anglaise" as a disguised way of saying he is tired of her,

METROLAND

though this is not what Christopher thinks he is confessing, and as usual she seems to be right.

Marion is a more straightforward person, more skeptical and in her own way, like Annick, much more mature than Christopher. This comes out most clearly in their conversation about marriage and relationships that precedes the *éclaircissement* (and rupture) with Annick: a conversation in which she shocks him by insisting that while marriage is the normal, expected thing, she is unromantic about marital happiness and perhaps even about love. Her explanation for why people get married (in response to Christopher's vague idea that it comes about when you find the right girl at the right time) is "Opportunity, meal ticket, desire for children . . . fear of ageing, possessiveness. . . . I think it often comes from a reluctance to admit that you've never in your life loved hard enough to end up married. A sort of misplaced idealism, really, a determination to prove that you're capable of the ultimate experience" (116). Whatever expectations about marriage to Marion this conversation may set up, when part 3, set back in Metroland in 1977, begins, they are married.

The point of this section seems to be to show what it means to be grown up. In quick résumé, it appears that Christopher married Marion, despite Toni's jeering against marriage as bourgeois selling-out; that he is middle-class (of course, he has really always been middle-class but is no longer pretending to be in revolt); and that after a short period as a supply (that is, substitute) teacher he went to work in an advertising agency, inventing campaigns for washing products, then moved over into a publishing company handling the sorts of books he would once have despised—books about food and kitchens.

UNDERSTANDING JULIAN BARNES

Much of the contrast between what the youth imagined as himself in the future—a flaneur, a poet in residence at a nudist colony, a rebel—and what he is now is framed in conversations with Toni, who stubbornly refuses to see the point. Toni boycotts the wedding, sending instead a long argument against the institution of marriage and taking offense at Christopher's not having read it. Toni remains involved in fringe poetry and radical politics and is entirely scornful of Christopher's accommodation to the world of bourgeois commerce, of all things. Toni is an unsuccessful poet, and usually proud of it; Christopher writes a book about the mass transport around London—exploiting all those hours on the train from Metroland during his school years—which is published successfully. To Toni, compromise with the public to make his own writing sell would be contemptible, though he is bitter against the book buyers who ignore him. Christopher's production of nonfiction books on the details of bourgeois life appears, from the perspective represented by Toni (and the young Christopher), like a complete collapse of artistic and social conscience.

Three important things happen in the final section that put a sort of seal on Christopher's adult relations to death, sex, and art. One is that his Uncle Arthur dies; Arthur has been a comic figure, featured in the adolescent chapters. Returning from his cremation, Christopher realizes that his fear of death is gone.

A new willingness to contemplate his own death becomes a factor in his adjustment regarding sex. Wondering if he will in fact (as Toni has jeered) remain faithful to one woman until he dies, he spends some time considering infidelity, and in fact, as a result of flirting mildly with a woman at a party, receives an unmistakable invitation to an affair. Having rejected it, he tells Marion about it, expecting congratulations. Her response is far more unsettling: first, a calm statement that "of course" he will be unfaithful some time; then the declaration that she has had an affair, which he has never suspected. After some rather forced levity by way of making up, he reflects, "Perhaps it really was all all right?" (163). Here Barnes inaugurates the theme of cuckoldry that will figure again and again in his novels. It is not the pivot of the book, but the revelation and Christopher's way of reacting to it are important parts of the coming-of-age—or perhaps coming-to-terms—plot of *Metroland.*

The final surrender, if that is what it is, to middle-class, middle-aged suburban normality comes when Christopher attends an old-boys' dinner for his former school. All his old scorn for the school, for the kinds of "success" his classmates have found, for the masters, tugs at him; Toni sneers at him; but he goes along anyway, overcomes his instincts and enjoys himself, and is offered a job: setting up a new publishing imprint for translations of French classics.

Nothing about this final section, even though a job publishing French classics is a partial recovery of his old ambition (note that the translations are nonetheless a compromise with the mass public; the real cognoscenti should be able to read French), is treated as a triumph; Toni is always there as the voice of conscience, or undimmed youthful radicalism, or Puritanical suspiciousness of mammon, or urban contempt for the suburban values of Metroland. There is no suggestion that a life devoted to art and relentlessly opposed to the delusions of the bourgeoisie is wrong; but there is, all the same, a recognition that life does not usually work that way. In the final chapter he decides not to feel guilty about his material comforts (not riches: just things like central heating and carpeted floors) and his family, and he reflects "I'd call myself a happy man . . . I wonder why happiness is despised nowadays . . ." (174). David Leon Higdon comments, perhaps too sweepingly, "Chris, a limited but not untrustworthy narrator, is the last happy man in Barnes's novels."[4] Does this happiness arise from willingness to settle for less? Yes, to an extent.

Metroland is a remarkable first novel. The management of tone is one of the most impressive features: the tone of an older, wiser, more ordinary man looking back on the youth he once was; a man recounting the ironic way his life has turned out; a man who tells the story of a successful growing up and an essentially happy life. All this works without any trace of mawkishness or smugness. The ironic verbal texture, particularly of the first and second sections, keeps the tone astringent. The uncompromising Toni and the resolutely unsentimental Marion balance out the romantic side of Christopher.

For a short novel it is rich in ideas. Here France is an idea, as well as a style, a language, a pose, an image of the right sort of life, and a rebuke to Metroland. This idea (like almost everything else from the fifteen-year-old Christopher Lloyd's repertoire of convictions) must be adjusted as a result of experience. Living in France and having a French lover change the idea. So does the discovery that other English people also speak French and understand French painting but lack the awe toward France of Christopher and Toni. Dave, who is half French, has a little routine in which he is a Frenchman with limited English, saying things such as "Eep eep ourah . . . Tott'en'am 'Ot-spure. Mi-chel

Ja-zy. Bobb'ee Moiré" (about English footballers) or "Redon. Oxfor', Bah-nbri, Bur-meeng'am. *Changez, changez*" (109–10). The point of the joke, as Christopher does not see, is that the French can also be dazzled by English culture.

The idea of art is held up for examination as well. Christopher is never really an artist; he and Toni spend time in the museum, as adolescents, mostly as an exercise in the depreciation of other people's taste. In Paris he does a bit of writing, but his later account of that makes it clear that it is simply pastiche Baudelaire:

> urban allegories, sardonic character-sketches, elusive verse, and passages of straight descriptions, which gradually built up into the portrait of a city, a man, and—who could say?— perhaps a bit more. Their inspiration was openly acknowledged in the title, but it wasn't a question of imitation or parody, I explained to myself; it was more a question of trading on resonances, that most twentieth-century of techniques. (126)

His title *Spleenters* is indicative. No matter how he might wish to be, Christopher Lloyd is no melancholiac; he knows little or nothing about spleen.

This is a novel, then, that presents in all its potential interestingness the growth of a would-be *homme revolté,* or rebel, to an *homme moyen sensual,* an average sensual man; but this change is accompanied by very little of the disgust or acerbity which, in the modern novel, usually accompany that accommodation. It would be excessive to call this novel antimodernist, but *Metroland* displays a considerable skepticism toward the "religion of art" characteristic of moderns such as Joyce and even Barnes's beloved Flaubert; and its acceptance of suburbia, that nightmare for T. S. Eliot and Virginia Woolf, also removes it from the mainstream of modernist attitudes.[5] It is a courageous book. Julian Barnes has enough of Toni in him to know that, to some readers, *Metroland* is going to be "a prig's progress."[6] Art is about that sort of courageousness far more than about how to *épater la bourgeoisie* or *écraser l'infame*.

CHAPTER THREE

Duffy

If Julian Barnes has been devotedly pursuing difference and freedom from the conventional expectations of the English novel in his mainstream fictions, in the Duffy books he does something almost exactly opposite. Not only are the four books similar to each other, but they are similar to other detective novels. Though this resemblance to a norm is avoidable, it is what is meant when people describe detective novels as formula fiction, or genre fiction: they operate within a more narrowly inscribed radius of variation than other types of novel. For instance, readers of detective fiction can almost always expect with confidence that the crime will be solved; mystification followed by explanation is part of the promise of this sort of text. The criminal may not be punished or may only be punished irregularly (perhaps by Duffy) rather than through the official system of criminal justice; but readers can expect that they will not be left with an unexplained crime. A detective novel is not quite the same as a mystery novel; but in each there is some puzzle, some thing which neither the reader nor the main character knows; and in each that puzzle must be cleared up by the end of the novel.

In the Duffy books Barnes seems to be enjoying a holiday from the usual expectations of art fiction or "serious" fiction. Richard Brown has speculated on his motives for writing detective books:

> In the contemporary fiction scene a successful high-brow novel may well outsell a supposedly "popular" crime

thriller, so profit alone is not sufficient motive. The Duffy novels helped give Barnes some street-credibility and may also have served to keep his desire to be sensational out of mainstream fiction.[1]

These distinctions—highbrow, "mainstream" fiction as opposed to sensational, supposedly "popular" crime thrillers—deserve some attention. As Brown points out, though crime fiction is often included in the "popular" category, it is not necessarily any more popular, in the sense of selling many books, than "mainstream" fiction. In another sense, popular meaning "of the people," it is. Without question, books that fit into the "genre fiction" category—science fiction, detective and mystery fiction, romances, cowboy novels—occupy an uneasy and ambiguous place in the world of books. Simply put, they lack prestige. They have been strenuously defended by many readers and writers; respected mainstream novelists such as Kingsley Amis have written genre fiction—in Amis's case spy novels, science fiction, and two detective novels; other esteemed "literary" writers such as Peter Ackroyd have written genre fiction, though often with an ironic, distancing twist. Furthermore, in the case of the mystery, there is ample evidence that respected artists both read them and write them. Still, the "popular" genres occupy something of a literary ghetto. Barnes, despite his ambitions and abilities in mainstream, literary fiction, has thought enough of the detective thriller to write four of them, four very good ones.

Nevertheless, they were published under a pseudonym. There are many possible reasons for this decision, including the one he provides: not wanting confusion between the two parts of his career, he assigned them two different names. It is significant, though, that the pseudonym went on the detective books and Barnes's real name on his "high-brow" novels. Likewise, Doris Lessing's series of science fiction books initially appeared under a pseudonym. (In each case the real authorship became known fairly quickly.)

Another insight into the difference between the mainstream books and the Duffy books comes from their different publishing histories. *Metroland* appeared in 1980 in England and was published in 1981 by St. Martin's Press in the United States; thereafter, each of Barnes's mainstream novels has been almost immediately, or simultaneously, published in New York by a major publisher, recently Alfred A. Knopf; the only exception is *Before She Met Me* (1982), not published in America until 1986 (that is, after the success of *Flaubert's Parrot*). The experience of the Duffy books is much more spotty. *Duffy* (1980) and *Fiddle City* (1981) were not published in this country until 1986, when they appeared in the Pantheon International Crime series as paperback originals. *Going to the Dogs* achieved an American hardback publication simultaneous with its English appearance (1987). *Putting the Boot In* (1985) has never been published in the United States. One obvious explanation for this lapse is its setting in the world of professional soccer, which is alien to most American readers; while this may be true, professional soccer is certainly no more a stranger to the U.S. reading public than are the details of Gustave Flaubert's life and works, or reformist politics in Bulgaria, or life on the Metropolitan line of the London Underground. A glance at the publication record, like a reflection on the use of the name Dan Kavanagh, reinforces the class division between mainstream, or highbrow, or literary novels and the popular (implicitly lowbrow, though that is unfair) novels of detection and crime.

Whatever his reason for writing them, he also seems to have enjoyed the opportunity to invent alternative biographies for his pseudonym Dan Kavanagh. For *Duffy* the account reads:

> Dan Kavanagh was born in County Sligo in 1946. Having devoted his adolescence to truancy, venery and petty theft, he left home at seventeen and signed on as a deckhand on a Liberian tanker. After jumping ship at Montevideo, he roamed across the Americas taking a variety of jobs: he was a steer-wrestler, a waiter-on-roller-skates at a drive-in eaterie in Tuscon [*sic*], and a bouncer at a gay bar in San Francisco. He is currently working in London at jobs he declines to specify, and lives in North Islington.

Particularly compared to Barnes's background—private school, Oxford, and the editorial staff of the *Times Literary Supplement*—this is louche. For *Fiddle City* the facts have changed, though the tone is the same; here it is claimed that he has been a "pianist in a waterfront bar in Macao, a baggage handler at San Francisco International Airport, and has flown light planes on the Colombian cocaine route." For *Putting the Boot In* the life has changed again: now Kavanagh, at seventeen, "signed apprentice forms with Accrington Stanley F.C., but was released by the club shortly afterwards." Accrington Stanley is a famous hard-luck, in fact defunct, football club.

DUFFY

Barnes's character Duffy is much more like fictional American detectives of the hard-boiled school associated with author Raymond Chandler than like, say, Hercule Poirot or Miss Marple or Roderick Alleyn.[2] The single name (Duffy's other name, seldom used, is Nick), the identifying idiosyncracies (Duffy's habitual neatness, his hatred of the sound of clocks or watches), the marginal existence, the alienation and estrangement—all these place Barnes's Duffy firmly in the hard-boiled tradition. Duffy is alienated by his ambiguous position in the world of crime; a former police detective who lost his job as a result of a frame-up engineered when he threatened criminals friendly with the police, he now works as a security consultant—a job that readily leads him into crime solving as a way of discovering whom he is providing security against. Still on the side of the police—or at least opposed to the criminals—and frequently mistaken for a policeman, he is nevertheless mistrusted by the force. He occupies a legal shadowland.

His isolation is even more pronounced because of his bisexuality. Duffy's sexual situation and its associated woes occupy a large place in the four books. Though a bisexual who has frequent casual affairs with men, he is in love with a fellow officer named Carol. A passage that fills in Duffy's history before the events chronicled in *Duffy* explains how his bisexuality is connected with his former-policeman status. When he threatened to arrest the wrong people in investigating a prostitute's stabbing in Soho, fellow policemen entrapped him in a homosexual liaison with a young man allegedly under the age of consent. The penalty was the loss of his job, the disruption of his relationship with Carol, and a growing cynicism. While he has restored friendly relations with Carol, and they sometimes spend the night together, Duffy is impotent with her (for whom he cares) but with no one else. The relationship with Carol, their jealousy of each other (Duffy knows Carol must be seeing other men but tries not to object), their professional entanglements (Duffy's need to get police files and computer access from Carol)—all these make for a somewhat messy background to Duffy's detection.

Finally, and in this also like classic fictional private eyes, Duffy is both finely ethical and legally slippery. He breaks into buildings and commits other crimes, including arson, which are, however, in the pursuit of some larger good. Even as a policeman this firmly moral but not quite legalistic stance had guided his actions, as the narrator of *Duffy* explains:

> Duffy, like most coppers, had a slightly flexible approach to the truth. You had to if you wanted to survive: not survive as a copper, but survive within yourself.... Sometimes, for instance, it might be necessary to tell a little lie, fiddle your notebook [i.e. of evidence] just a bit, in order to make sure that a much bigger lie didn't get to pass itself off as the truth. On those occasions you felt bad for a bit, though you knew you didn't have any choice in the matter.
>
> But Duffy, like most coppers, knew that you always drew a line somewhere. You might tidy up your verbals a bit, fiddle your evidence slightly, forget a little something, but you always knew why you were doing it: you were fixing the record in favour of justice.[3]

This distinction between what official dishonesty is permissible and what is excessive, between what is done disinterestedly, "in favour of justice," and what is done selfishly, like bribe-taking, is both delicate and important to Duffy. It is a real moral code. In none of the books is his client completely innocent or completely honest; in none of them are the police public-spirited or trustworthy; but there is nevertheless a strong feeling of right and wrong, which Duffy serves in his own way.

Duffy, published in 1980, quickly sets the standard features of the whole Dan Kavanagh series. It starts rapidly with an opening that combines startling information, violence, and a deadpan tone implying that the narrator is more blasé, or worldly, about such things than might be expected.

> The day they cut Mrs. McKechnie, not much else happened in West Byfleet. Not much happened in Pyrford either, or even in the whole of Guildford. . . . So when they cut Mrs. McKechnie, you'd expect the *Advertiser*'s story on Page Seven to have led with this fact; but it didn't. It led with the other thing the men did, the afterthought, the nasty, sick thing which even Big Eddy, with his sense of humor, didn't really approve of. (7)

In general the level of violence in the Duffy books, while perhaps shocking to English readers, is fairly low by American standards. People are seldom killed, though animals sometimes are, and people are cut badly, burned, beaten up, and threatened with worse torments, including castration. The opening promises a level of ruthlessness that the book never actually delivers. The English paperback edition of *Duffy* sports a blurb from *Cosmopolitan* urging: "Take a deep breath and read it: it's brilliant, but it's double X-Certificate stuff." The X rating in Britain is more likely to be imposed for violence than for sex, which is, in fact, plentiful and raunchy in *Duffy*.

What happened to Mrs. McKechnie, as disclosed in a round-about first chapter, is that two men entered her home and tied her up, making it clear they were acting under specific orders; they mentioned "Barbara" (who later turns out to be Mr. McKechnie's mistress); they carefully sterilized a Stanley knife and cut Mrs. McKechnie in the back of the shoulder to a length of three inches—"The boss said three inches" (14). The only unplanned part of the attack, the afterthought, is when they put the cat into the spit-roaster oven and turned it to high. That this part, the barbarous treatment of a pet, is the lead in the local paper's coverage of "the day they cut Mrs. McKechnie" is an ironic commentary on the British press's sentimentality about animals.

The assault is followed shortly by the blackmailing of Mr. McKechnie, described as an importer of masks and other novel-ties with warehouses in Soho. The police show little inclination or ability to help him (the investigating officer describes the case to McKechnie, who has a criminal record, as "some local villain reads a Guildford newspaper and squeezes a pony out of another local fiddler" [30]). McKechnie brings in Duffy Security and thus, by a circuitous route, Duffy himself. What follows is a complicated plot in which little is what it initially seems: McKechnie is not really an importer of masks and novelties but a pornography merchant; his menacing blackmailer, identified as Salvatore, is really a Maltese criminal named Big Eddy Martoff; the police are not really trying at all to solve the McKechnie case but, under the leadership of the same corrupt or "bent" copper who ended Duffy's career on the force, are in league with Martoff.

The atmosphere throughout is of streetwise worldliness and casual menace. One major source of the tone is the slang. While Martoff, a second-generation villain who has a good education and expensive tastes, usually speaks in an elegant way, Duffy uses the slang of the police, to whom he refers as "the blues." A typical example of his discourse has him explaining that a criminal was "a medium-sized protection man; did a few smokes and tarts as well" (48). The police refer to their beat as their "patch," and Martoff explains that he is choosing his words carefully to make himself comprehensible to Duffy when he orders him to "Get off my patch" (122).

The menace of Martoff and his followers is usually only implied; when asked what he will do if his wishes are ignored (if McKechnie does not pay up, if Duffy does not stay off his patch), he answers, "suck it and see" (33, 122). But in the course of this novel the damage includes the cutting of Mrs. McKechnie, assaults on prostitutes, and arson by throwing paraffin (for example, kerosene) heaters through windows. Duffy, having ignored his warning, is entrapped in a massage parlor and threatened with emasculation, then further "neutralized" by another frameup, complete with photographs. The flavor of the novel is nasty, and the nastiness is emphasized by the euphemism, indirection, and formality of Martoff's dialogue and surroundings.

Duffy "solves" the case, gets a sort of revenge, partially neutralizes Martoff, and exposes the crooked policeman Sullivan. But he hardly triumphs. The moral atmosphere of

Duffy is ambiguous, the lines shifting, as a friendly policeman tries to explain:

> You know as well as I do that in a place like our patch there's always a delicate balance between us and the villains. It's not a great war like the public seems to imagine and it's not a lazy heap of coppers on the take like you seem to imagine. The villains and us carry on side by side and there's a sort of what you call osmosis between us. . . .
> You're upsetting this delicate balance, you see, Duffy. (130)

"Delicate balance" is actually a precisely descriptive phrase for what Duffy wants to achieve. At the end, he has partly negated Martoff and exposed the most corrupt members of the police. The balance had been upset by too much power in one set of hands. Clearly, the casual crime will continue: "punters" will pay tarts; small bribes and compromises will continue as before. But Duffy has intervened, reluctantly, into the process and restored it to something closer to the balance demanded by his moral code.

The next year Barnes/Kavanagh followed Duffy with *Fiddle City*. He has explained in response to a question about why he used a pseudonym, "I knew I wanted to write several thrillers and I didn't know what would come in what order, and I didn't want to be the author of *Metroland* and three thrillers all under the same name."[4] The pseudonym, clearly, was only for the thrillers, which may have seemed a bit of literary slumming, keeping his real name for his more slowly developing body of literary novels. *Fiddle City* is the villains' argot for Heathrow Airport; in this novel Duffy becomes involved in investigating a smuggling operation that also involves violence. In fact, the book opens with the act of violence, in a sentence that echoes the opening of *Duffy:* "The day they crashed McKay, not much else happened on the M4" (7). What follows is a detailed description of how two motorists acting in concert cause McKay to smash his custom- ized Cortina against the guard rail and an account, slightly sickening in its satisfaction, of the results: "McKay himself made a long red trail on the metal barrier in a way that no one could quite understand. . . . Why did it look as if someone or something had *smeared* the poor fellow all along the barrier?" (11–12). He isn't dead, though he is badly injured. The detail that he was picking his nose with something sharp at the time of the crash and nearly cut off his nose adds to the picture of horrible damage that still remains nonlethal. This is the sort of sensationalism that, what- ever the effect of the Kavanagh books in siphoning it off, almost never appears in Barnes's mainstream novels, *Before She Met Me* being the only real exception.

Barnes then, again as in *Duffy,* pursues a roundabout way of getting Duffy involved in the case. First Duffy has a one-night stand with a man named Eric whom he meets in his favorite gay bar, the Alligator, and this gives an opportunity for exposition of the Duffy persona: meticulous, intolerant of watches, watchful, working-class. Only when Eric returns to the Alligator a few weeks later and recruits Duffy to investigate a case of theft is the linkup between the detective and Heathrow and the McKay assault complete. Duffy will go to work in a warehouse at Heathrow, undercover; he is McKay's replacement.

What follows is the familiar combination of menace and confusion followed by insight. The menace comes from Duffy's coworkers, who threaten him, try to bribe him, and plant stolen goods in his car and alert the investigators; the confusion comes from his own uncertainty about what crime has been committed and by whom, and his discovery of a related arena of illicit activity, a strip bar reminiscent of *Duffy*, with which his icy and repellent supervisor Mrs. Boseley has some unexplained and improbable connection. Most of the insight, or at least information, comes from a friend, named Willett, who works as a customs inspector and who provides Duffy and the reader with explanations of smuggling tactics, how inspectors catch smugglers, and how they decide whom to search. Willett also helps to fill in the authoritative flavor of this novel, especially in language: he explains to Duffy, for instance, about "stuffers," women who try to carry in condoms full of heroin inserted into their bodies. Duffy once again uses the assistance of his friend Geoff Bell, the electronics expert who helped him with snooping devices in *Duffy*.

The villains win the first round, when the heroin smugglers realize Duffy is an impostor. He gets his revenge later on, at first physically—the heavy who has used pliers to jerk the stud from Duffy's left ear receives a thorough beating and, under the threat of being injected with a deadly dose of heroin, confesses the secrets Duffy needs. He manages to solve the small mystery— why was McKay smashed?—the slightly larger mystery for which he was hired—who is stealing from the warehouse?—and the much larger one, which only became apparent by degrees, having to do with a major heroin-smuggling operation.

Duffy is prim and absolute in his distaste for drug dealers. His relativism about crime is familiar; but his absolutism about drugs is one of the exceptions.

Duffy's moral outlook had always been pragmatic.
Three years in the force had made it more so, and it wasn't
going to change now. He wasn't idealistic about the law,
or about how it was implemented. He didn't mind a bit of
give-and-take, a bit of blind-eye, a bit of you-naughty-
boy-on-yer-bike and forget it. He didn't think the ends
justified the means—except that sometimes, just occasionally, they did. He didn't believe all crimes were equal;
some he couldn't get worked up about. But always, at the
back, there were absolutes. Murder was one, of course,
everyone agreed on that. Bent coppers was one; but then,
Duffy had a little private experience of that, and could be
expected to feel strongly. Rape was one; Duffy was
disgusted how some coppers thought it was little more
than a mild duffing up with a bit of pleasure thrown in. And
heroin was one as well. (101)

What follows is the story of Lesley, his addict friend: "At one end
of the chain there were dead babies in Thailand"—a reference to
Willett's tale of Asian women hollowing out babies for transport-
ing drugs over borders; "at the other end there were Lesleys fixing
themselves to death" (103).

There was a four-year gap between *Fiddle City* and the next
Duffy book. *Putting the Boot In* appeared in 1985, after *Before
She Met Me* and Barnes's first really acclaimed novel, *Flaubert's
Parrot*. The milieu this time is small-time professional football.
In this novel Barnes has made a few changes. One of them is
almost mandatory: Duffy, who has been a bisexual with a
moderately promiscuous sex life among men and (though to a

lesser extent) women, is now aware of AIDS and in fact is almost continually worried about it; he asks Carol to examine him for signs of Kaposi's sarcoma lesions, checks out his own lymph nodes on a regular basis, and has become celibate, though sharing a bed with Carol. This changes the atmosphere of the novel quite a bit.

Another change is the framing. The novel is set up in five parts: parts 1, 3, and 5 are called "Warm-Up," "Half-Time," and "Extra Time" and are really about a game of football played by the Western Sunday Reliables, a team for which Duffy keeps goal. This is an amusing glimpse of Duffy in action with his friends; he is as fastidious in goal tending as in his home life— "he liked the neat box of the penalty area; he liked the way it marked out his territory, his manor."[5] There is also a nice parallel that pivots on the expression "to keep a clean sheet"—that is, to permit the opposition no goals. Duffy has modest success as a goalkeeper but in his sex life has kept "a succession of clean sheets . . . when he was searching his legs for brown blotches and taking his temperature every other day; the time when the Alligator and all the other clubs were running scared" (16). Recurring character Geoff Bell, the electronics expert, is a member of the team; though he is a bad football player, his real skill is bugging the opposing team's dressing room in order to learn their plans.

In "Warm-Up" Duffy finds himself thinking about Danny Matson. His first thoughts are, "There are too many ways of breaking a footballer's leg" (11). This is the link to the main story, told in retrospect as Duffy thinks about it during his own football game and divided into the two long sections of the novel, "First Half" and "Second Half."

DUFFY

As usual the beginning is an act of violence—in this case a woman has picked up promising midfielder Danny Matson in a bar and lured him into a car park where someone breaks his leg, ending his career. Duffy is brought in by Danny's manager at the struggling Third Division team Athletic to help watch over the team. Manager Lister is presiding over a team on the edge: threatened by relegation (being dropped into the Fourth Division, the lowest branch of the Football League). Lister is afraid of his owner Melvyn Prosser, baffled by his team's problems, and, as Duffy realizes, not actually any good as a manager. The loss of Danny Matson, one of his two good players, makes things look darker, and there are many other apparently unrelated problems threatening the team: the rise of a large and vocal following of neofascist thugs, who scare off fans, incur increased costs in policing, and harass the team's only black player, who after Danny's injury is now the only star; declining financial fortunes, which will only become worse if the team is relegated; and an oddly timed lawsuit by neighbors of the club's stadium who object to the noise and disruption caused by the supporters. The other shoe falls when Brendan Domingo, the black player and the remaining hope, is offered a bribe, which he rejects, and is then seduced by a woman in a bar and accused of rape and battery.

Duffy's investigations turn up one other fact: an application for planning permission to redevelop the football ground as something else. It is in the name of an old friend of the owner Prosser, now apparently an enemy.

This is a case Duffy never really *solves*. With the help of Geoff Bell he identifies the girl who framed Domingo and set up Matson and removes her as a threat; he gets Domingo freed to play in the last three games, in which Athletic manages to escape relegation; and he puts all the clues together to discover that Melvyn Prosser, supposed savior of Athletic, has actually been the one trying to ruin it—by encouraging the thugs, encouraging the neighbors' suit, disabling his best players, even deliberately hiring an incompetent manager under whom the team would naturally fail. When Duffy accuses Prosser of all this he receives a bland denial.

Unlike the rough sorting out of right and wrong that Duffy achieves in *Duffy* and *Fiddle City,* the denouement here is ambiguous and deeply ironic. The team avoids relegation and is sold by Prosser to a real football fan, after which they play terribly and (in the following season) are almost certainly destined for disaster. Brendan Domingo, having saved his team, fakes an attack by Athletic fans and is able to break his contract and leave the team to play somewhere better. No one is ever prosecuted for anything, and Duffy ends as he began, by thinking ruefully about Danny Matson, whose career is over:

> A dozen first-team games, a sniff of the big time, free entry to The Knight Spot, striking up an understanding with big Brendan, photo in the papers, popular with the girls, waiting delivery on the new Capri, and then . . . *phut.* You're a small feature in somebody else's plans and your career goes down the toilet. Never knowing why, never knowing who. Left with a few thoughts about football being a cruel game and a folded picture of Trevor Brooking's room. Where was Danny Matson now? (192)

DUFFY

The changes in *Putting the Boot In* may be construed as showing Barnes's impatience with the standard format (Duffy puts things more or less to rights) as well as a sobered awareness of the consequences of his detective's sex life. Moreover, the more complex, artful construction of this novel, with the "real" story of Duffy, Athletic, and Danny Matson a past event filtered through sections of a "present" football game and cleverly paced to the segments of a match, also suggests that the formula may have come to feel too constricting.

In *Going to the Dogs* the dissatisfaction with the Duffy series—the feeling that, as Richard Brown argues, "the joke and the material have been wearing a little thin"[6]—comes out in a more labored production, as well as in some inside jokes. The milieu here is not one downmarket world, carefully delineated, like the Soho sex industry, Heathrow, or south London professional football; instead, it is the world of the very rich, newly inhabited by a former villain known to Duffy, with a secondary scene of London dog racing in the south London working-class area from which the former villain has risen.

This is the most complicated of the Duffy books, with a tangled plot involving rich decadents, repressed homosexuality among the gentry, drugs, and suicide. It is also the most class-conscious; in it Duffy, who has always been clearly marked as working-class, comes up against the upper classes. These are not just the wealthy—many villains are wealthy, including Vic Crowther, the customer whose alarm system Duffy has installed in his Home Counties mansion—but the people who are reared in privilege—for whom Vic has become an unwilling host—are different: spoiled, snobbish, smug, and degenerate. The case brings out Duffy's hostilities.

> He tried saying poor kid to himself as he hitchhiked round the Hall looking for her; but he wasn't really convinced. Poor kid for what happened up in the woods, sure. Poor kid for the life she led, sorry, nothing doing. Duffy didn't soften at the sufferings of the rich. He'd heard about them often enough, he'd seen them all the time in American soap operas on the telly; but he didn't buy the package. People with money didn't have the right to whinge, that's what Duffy thought.[7]

In each of the Duffy books he has some difficulty sympathizing with his client—because the client is shady himself, as in *Duffy* or *Fiddle City,* or because he is hapless and something of a born victim, as in *Putting the Boot In.* Here he likes his client, Vic, because of his background; he simply cannot muster much sympathy for the victims, because of their background. In *Putting the Boot In* there is a feeling of hostility toward the world of amoral businessmen such as Melvyn Prosser, who coldly uses working-class people like the football players, the football supporters, and Duffy himself. Here the class resentment is more firmly articulated.

Going to the Dogs begins with another indirect opening and another act of violence.

> There was a body in the video library. It was hard to miss, as these things are, and Mrs. Colin spotted it the

moment she pushed open the panelled light-oak door on which someone had humorously painted a large pink trompe-l'oeil keyhole. Mrs. Colin recognized Ricky at once, recognized equally that he was dead, and put her hand to her throat. (11)

It is some pages before the narration reveals that Ricky is a dog, hurled through a window as a warning or punishment to its owner, who is being blackmailed. The deliberate confusion of the scale of violence, and the extremity of response, between assaults on people and animals is a reminder of the beginning of *Duffy*, where the cutting of Mrs. McKechnie is subordinated in the press to the grilling of a cat.

The next chapter, which makes the customary linkup with Duffy, is much more roundabout than usual, devoting a good many pages to Duffy's doing his wash at a launderette, his mundane reflections on lost socks, his tastes in breakfast, some light comic relief about a Chinese café owner named Sam Widges because he once specialized in sandwiches, and much more. When he returns to his flat it becomes clear that Duffy is with Carol again before the call from Vic summons him to the scene of the crime.

This playful exposition of unimportant parts of Duffy's personality—like his football playing in *Putting the Boot In*—this refusal to hew to the rigidities of the detective format, may be a symptom of Barnes's growing impatience with the Duffy pattern. Another symptom, especially as contextualized by Duffy's AIDS fears in *Putting the Boot In*, is what seems to be Duffy's growing interest in women (here he reflects that he has had "quite a spell of being queer" [84], though it is not clear when this ended). One of the youthful rich, with whom he is generally out of sympathy, nevertheless appeals to him sexually. As he tries to chat her up, Lucretia puts him in his place by reference to the world she moves in, specifically by informing him, "I'm reading a fairly good restaurant critic called Basil Seal in a magazine called the *Tatler*. I don't suppose that's part of your regular culture" (60). This has the desired effect on Duffy of silencing him and causing resentment, as shown by the explanation "Lucretia returned to Basil Berk writing about the Golden Sausage in the *Wankers' Monthly*" (60). Duffy resents not only Lucretia but Basil Seal himself; later he reads the following month's *Tatler* and thinks:

> What was Basil Berk writing about this month? Duffy read the page with rising incredulity. Call this a job? You went along to some wallies' rendezvous—in the present case one of three fish restaurants in Chelsea—had a jolly good nosh-up, took Lady Berk along with you, copied down the menu, made up some joke or other and pretended Lady Berk had said it to you across the fish-knives and went on to the next restaurant. And the prices . . . You could get seven good dinners at Sam Widges for the prices of a single fish snack in Chelsea. (84)

But this is also a long inside joke, since the restaurant critic writing as Basil Seal in the *Tatler* was in fact Julian Barnes, who has explained that "I suppose in a way it was another fictional voice. Basil had a lot of terrible prejudices and didn't care what he said."[8] There are other little self-references in this book, or at least references to the other Duffy books—the killing of Ricky is specifically linked to the case in Soho where "something very nasty" was done to a cat. Lucretia, who warms to Duffy a bit, tells him that she does not like football because of "All that putting the boot in" (174).

All these are added to the use of the title as a leitmotif—various characters complain that the country is "going to the dogs," which is not only a reference to Ricky's death but to Duffy and Carol's visit to the dog track and their realization there that some gamblers disable their own dogs and bet against them, a realization which, by analogy, helps Duffy to figure out who killed Ricky. Together they make *Going to the Dogs* the most consciously artistic, the most witty, the most self-aware of the Duffy series. This makes it the least satisfying crime thriller and evidently helps to explain why there have been no more Duffy books, only works of literary fiction in which such art is an important and expected part of the book, not an indulgence or a distraction.

CHAPTER FOUR

Before She Met Me

In his second mainstream novel Julian Barnes displays, for the first time, a radically distinctive voice and flair; he begins to explore, in depth, what is arguably his central network of subjects—love, infidelity, and jealousy; and he writes with a mixture of the comic and the macabre, the lurid and the jocose, which invites comparisons with his friends and contemporaries, Martin Amis and Ian McEwan.

If *Metroland* told the story of how a boy who thought he was extraordinary grew up to be an ordinary man, *Before She Met Me* tells of an ordinary man becoming extraordinary, in a terrible way. Christopher Lloyd, who likes to think of himself as a sophisticated tough, accommodates himself to ordinary life and marriage, even a marriage which he discovers has been flawed by his wife's infidelity, with surprising readiness. Graham Hendrick, whose profession of university lecturer seems chosen almost as shorthand for "stodgy, unadventurous, incapable of strong emotion," begins by leaving his wife in an uncharacteristically forceful but lighthearted way and ends by committing savage murder. It would be glib, perhaps, to describe *Before She Met Me* as combining the social observation, comedy, and verbal dexterity of *Metroland* with the queasy moral atmosphere and proximity to violence of *Duffy;* but some such merging seems to have taken place.

The comparison with McEwan and Amis is instructive.[1] Amis was born in 1949, McEwan in 1948, Barnes in 1946. Amis published his first novel, the prizewinning *The Rachel Papers,* in 1973; McEwan attracted important critical attention with the publication of his first book of short stories, *First Love, Last Rites,* in 1975. Barnes had begun his writing career under the influence of the younger, and famously precocious, Martin Amis, working as his subordinate on both the *Times Literary Supplement* and *The New Statesman.* Both Amis and McEwan had earned reputations, in their fiction, for choosing extreme situations and outrageous developments, narrated with a combination of studied nonchalance and sometimes shocking humor (Amis's title *Dead Babies*—which was changed to *Dark Secrets* for one reprint—suggests the tone). A novel such as McEwan's *The Cement Garden* (1978), in which a family of four children bury their mother (dead of natural causes) in the basement and live an increasingly bizarre, dreamlike life, complete with transvestitism and brother-sister incest, certainly pushes the boundaries of the postwar middle-class literary novel. *Before She Met Me* is another such novel of unease, growing menace, and mental disturbance. Barnes himself calls it "a rather nasty book about unpleasant sexual feelings, jealousies and obsessions. It was meant to have had a rather sour and hard-driving edge to it. I think it's my funniest book, though the humor is rather bleak and in bad taste usually."[2] He is right: it is a very funny book. Writing a book this funny which nevertheless turns out to be this savage, without tonal inconsistency or unintended humor, is quite an impressive accomplishment.

As is most fitting for a novel about adultery and jealousy and an author as fond of the French tradition as Barnes is, the characters in *Before She Met Me* are arranged in a series of triangles. There is a classical simplicity to the relationship among the four main characters, two men and two women. The protagonist, Graham Hendrick, is an academic in his late thirties who, caught up in a stale marriage to an unpleasant woman, meets an exciting new woman and falls in love with her. Graham teaches twentieth-century British political history at the University of London; his profession seems to matter little to him and, aside from (perhaps) being an authorial indication of Graham's timidity and lack of adventure, functions mostly as a job that gives Graham plenty of free time to pursue his obsessions.

It also provides a contrast with Ann Mears, the young woman with whom Graham falls in love and whom he marries. Ann is a clothes buyer; more important, as it turns out, is her previous career as an unsuccessful actress, during which she appeared in small roles in many forgettable films. Though intelligent and interested in reading and travel, Ann is no intellectual. On the other hand, she is far more experienced than Graham in most worldly ways. In an account of the early days of their affair, the narrator explains,

> She felt, at the same time, both older and younger than him. Sometimes she pitied him for the narrowness of his previous life; at others she felt daunted by the thought that she would never know as many things as Graham, would never be able to argue with the directness and logic which she perceived in him. On occasions, lying in bed, she found herself thinking about his brain.[3]

BEFORE SHE MET ME

The contrast between husband and wife provides some grounds for associating Graham with the traditional cuckold type, as Mark Millington and Alison Sinclair delineate it:

> In certain ways Graham fits the model of the cuckold quite
> clearly: he is variously described as wet (77), as a "weed"
> (70), and (connoting his age) as virtually retired at thirty-
> eight (12). And his weakness is contrasted with the evident
> knowledge and mastery shown by Ann, especially in the
> area of sex: Ann's earlier independent life stands in stark
> contrast to the limitations of Graham's previous experi-
> ence in his first marriage.[4]

The third member of the original triangle is Graham's first wife, Barbara. Though there is little reason to believe that she loves Graham, and their sex life has been arid and unsatisfying for years, she makes an enormous tragedy of his leaving and the aftermath, including many demands on him financially and a cruel and canny campaign to turn his daughter Alice against him. The most thoroughly thought-out tactic in this campaign produces the complication in the plot that drives this novel, since it produces the second triangular relationship, or more accurately, the second and third.

Barbara persuades Graham to take Alice to see an obscure film, claiming that Alice particularly wants to see it because it features her school; in reality she has somehow discovered that the film includes Ann in a small role as an adulteress. This explains the beginning of the novel, which, as usual for Barnes, is pithy and intriguing: "The first time Graham Kendrick watched his wife commit adultery he didn't mind at all. He even found himself chuckling. It never occurred to him to reach out a shielding hand towards his daughter's eyes" (9). The daughter, whom Barbara had prepared to see one of Ann's "most convincing screen roles," declares that Ann was "such a *tart*" (30) in the film, and Graham, reasonably enough, tries to persuade her to remember the difference between the actress and the role.

This is a distinction Graham almost immediately loses control over in his own mind. In talking over the film with Ann, he learns that she had in fact had a real-life affair with the actor with whom she had pretended to have an affair in the film. This is the inciting event that precipitates everything else that happens in the book, which is a ruthlessly worked out development of Graham's jealousy of men who, in life or in the movies or both, had affairs with his wife "before she met me."

This triangle, then, is flexible—the third side, or party, changes frequently—and mostly in Graham's mind. He knows this; but knowing it does not prevent him from becoming more and more extreme, ridiculous, and fanatical in his devotion to discovering Ann's previous lovers. He travels all over London to watch films Ann appeared in briefly, some of which she has herself forgotten; he develops an almost photographic memory of whom Ann has slept with, whether on the screen or not, and in fact challenges her at one point to quiz him on the subject. After some time he finds himself going to movies Ann was not in when there are men in them with whom she has acted in the past, and he even videotapes television commercials in which these actors appear. He spends much of his time looking through film listings in newspapers and traveling around London to see obscure movies, often again and again.[5]

This obsession is in many ways a predictable development from Graham's previous, and presumably more acceptable, obsession with Ann. Testifying to how much he loves her, he explains that he always writes down in his diary, from memory, what she wears to work every day and

> "I get out my diary—sometimes when I'm teaching and pretend to be thinking about essay titles or something—and I sit there, sort of dressing her. It's very . . . nice.
>
> I'll tell you another thing. I always clear the table after dinner. I go through to the kitchen, and I scrape my plate off into the kitchen bin, and then I suddenly find myself eating whatever she's left on hers. Often, you know, it isn't anything particularly nice—bits of fat and discoloured vegetables and sausage gristle—but I just scoff it." (51)

Graham Hendrick tries to be a reasonable man, and he knows that his obsession with his wife's past is unreasonable. She has never made any attempt to hide her sexual experience nor to flaunt it; she answers truthfully his questions about whether or not she has slept with her fellow actors. She is bemused and saddened by his growing fixation.

The painful triangular relationship between Graham, his wife, and her past "lovers" (most of them imaginary) is particularly painful because there are a large number of the latter, including good-looking actors; because Graham has nothing to retaliate with, having little sexual history of his own; because, knowing that he is unreasonable, he can neither feel justified in his jealousy nor stop feeling it; and because, since the occasions for the jealousy are all in the past, there is nothing anybody can do about them. In a newspaper column on jealousy, Barnes has this to say about jealousy of the past:

> Retro-jealousy, unlike its more familiar siblings, habitually broadens out into a wider obsession. That previous affair, that earlier lover turn out to be mere nominees for wider areas of baffled resentment: a kind of foolish rage against the immutability of the past, and a metaphysical whinge that things can actually happen despite your absence.[6]

Graham can find no satisfactory way of accommodating his knowledge. Avoidance might appear to be a sensible course; instead, by repeatedly watching the films and insisting on discussing the men with Ann, he wallows in his jealousy. On the other hand, avoidance becomes a need—and a problem—when they plan a trip to the Continent. Graham does not want to go anywhere with Ann that she has been with another lover; in a reflective mood, gazing at the map, he realizes that by traveling there with Ann, a certain Benny has spoiled much of Italy for him:

> He might as well take a pair of scissors to the map, shear straight across it from Pisa to Rimini, cut a parallel line through Assisi, and then stick the bottom bit of Italy back on to what was now left of the top bit. Make it into a

mere bootee—the sort with little buttons down the side. As
worn by posh whores; or so he imagined.

They could go to Ravenna, he supposed. He hated
mosaics. He really hated mosaics. Benny had left him with
the mosaics. Thanks very much, Benny. (55)

Ann comments, sadly, on the same process: "We're trying to find
some country where I haven't fucked someone" (68). When it
looks as if all of southern Europe will be off-limits, Graham
"imagined himself in one of those fringe countries, anoraked
against the cold and sipping a glass of goat's-hoof liquor; all there
would be to do was brood chippily on the easy, sun-tanned shits
who had driven him there and who were even now lolling down
the Via Veneto and mocking the thought of him" (98).

These remarks illustrate the comedy of this book, which
survives the harrowing content. Both Ann and Graham are often,
and increasingly, sad; and the book is often sad; but it is funny as
well. The results of Graham's growing obsession are originally
imagined and amusing. For instance, in avoiding, even mentally,
those parts of the world where Ann has been with another man,
he develops an exaggerated interest in the "safe" parts of the
world, reading more and more, for instance, about India, where
Ann has never gone with a lover, and beginning to babble to his
colleagues about the financial losses of Narita airport. Convinced
that he must be accurate in his jealousy, he finds out as much as
possible about his "rivals"; for instance, one of them, Jed, owned
a Range Rover; another, Michael, is said by Ann to have had "an
engaging way of shaking his head and blinking shyly at you" (61).

In his mind they become "the creep with the jeep" and "the prick with the tic" (60–61).

Among his other symptoms, Graham suffers from "sneering dreams," lurid, imaginative creations involving actors and Ann. The first summons up Buck Skelton, an American actor who was in *The Rattler and the Rubies* with Ann; in the dream he tells Graham in excruciating detail about his practices with Ann and how abandoned she was. The results of these dreams are significant enough: he busies himself with violent revenge fantasies and even enacts some sort of real revenge when he cuts up butcher's offal and mails it to unidentified enemies. What is more interesting is the reason for the dreams. Since he has no reason to believe that Ann has slept with either Skelton or Pitter, and has no reason to think that the wild sexual practices he has dreamed for her to enjoy with them actually hold any appeal for her, he has lost his moorings in reality—that is, jealousy and resentment of real affairs with real men—and filmed reality—that is, pretended affairs with actors in movies—and is now providing himself with pornographic images based in nothing but his own need to imagine and worry. That there is something masochistic about them is amply proved by his pain in dreaming them; but there is also something lubricious, something he likes. He knows his own ambivalence; earlier, while prowling through Ann's possessions looking for "evidence," he has "wondered whether he didn't secretly enjoy finding that proof which he told himself he feared and hated" (59).

The discussion so far has gone no further than Graham's obsessive resentment of a triangular relationship between himself, his wife, and rivals who are either in the past, in the movies, or in his mind. Thus *Before She Met Me* seems a study in paranoia, exaggeration and unjustified sexual worry. What complicates this picture and sends it diving toward tragedy is the real triangular relationship, involving Graham, Ann, and the fourth major character of the novel, Jack Lupton, successful novelist, friend and confidant to both Ann and Graham, accomplished adulterer in his own right, and a real living former lover to Ann.

Jack figures here in a variety of roles. He is the person who has introduced Graham and Ann, at a party at his house. He is also good for comic relief. A self-created "character," bluff and hearty, he has somehow given himself permission to pass wind publicly as a staple of his sense of humor; he has a winning line in picking up women, involving sticking his cigarette in his beard and pretending to forget it is there; he is, in British slang, "laddish," that is, hearty, crude, funny, and lecherous. He is also a steady source of information and advice about adultery. In fact *Before She Met Me* is filled with bits of advice about adultery. Jack explains the Parking Fine Principle, which is that confessing to the most recent infidelity may cause all the ones before to be erased from the memory, and his "rule about affairs: maximum deception, minimum lying, maximum kindness" (66). Jack's wife Sue helps fill out the syllabus, telling Graham about the Adulterer's Table at a very public restaurant, about the Stanley Spencer syndrome, named for the modern British painter—the artist's self-indulgence when it comes to sex—and about the "cancer rule. If they don't ask, you don't tell them; and if they do ask but really want to be told No, then you still say No" (159). All this fine, insouciant knowingness about adultery comes from Jack's sector of the novel.

As an expert on women and sex, Jack becomes Graham's adviser. He never takes this role particularly seriously, though he does advise Graham to have an affair himself, to masturbate, to learn to love his wife less. He becomes a confidant for Ann when she turns up one day to tell her side of the story of Graham's obsessions and to insist that she and Jack must rewrite history; she has decided that the two of them never had an affair (their real affair was, like all the others Graham worries about, in the past—Before She Met Me—but is now, given Graham's condition, far too dangerous to acknowledge).

This affair, suppressed as none of the others have been, is detected by Graham in his lapidary worrying over his findings (he gets his "clinching evidence" by reflecting on a bit of dialogue heard while "watching, for the third time that week, his wife committing onscreen adultery with Tony Rogozzi in *The Fool Who Found Fortune*" [147]), then worked up by a maniacal analysis of Jack's novels, all of which he finds to be filled with further evidence of the affair ("the more evidence Graham found, the easier it became to find yet more" [153]), which, on the basis of these clues, is "proven" to have continued all through his marriage. Graham is quite canny, in a crazed way, about the relation between truth and fiction, that recurrent question for Julian Barnes. He realizes that Jack—who does not seem to be a very good novelist, though this is hard to determine—lacks the imagination to make up his novels and must rely on disguised versions of his friends and altered retellings of his own life. Graham is on solid ground here; as he reads on, eager for the evidence he dreads, that Jack and Ann have been lovers during his marriage, he leaves that solid ground for mere delusions, though they seem evidence as soundly established in careful reading of the novels as they can be. This "discovery" finally drives Graham to extreme circumstances. As he sits in Jack's flat, waiting to commit an act of horrible violence, he reflects on the changes he has been through:

> In the old stories, people grew up, struggled, had misfortunes, and eventually came to ripeness, to a sense of being at ease with the world. Graham, after forty years of not struggling very much, felt he had come to ripeness in a few months, and irrevocably grasped that terminal unease was the natural condition. This sudden wisdom had disconcerted him at first; now he felt calm about it. As he pushed his hand into his jacket pocket, he admitted that he might be misunderstood; he might be thought of as merely jealous, merely crackers. Well, that was up to them. (162–63)

In addition to being a credible and compelling study of abnormal psychology, *Before She Met Me* is also a compelling study of normal psychology. The narrative focus, though more on Graham than anyone else, is distributed among the major characters; each is understood, and understandable, so that Barbara, even if fundamentally disagreeable, is a rounded character who does as she does for comprehensible reasons. The minds of Ann and Jack are more thoroughly revealed; their growing impatience with Graham, turning to disgust, despite initial sympathy, is artfully traced. Ann is a deep characterization, a complex woman, tested by the vagaries of the husband she loves.

UNDERSTANDING JULIAN BARNES

As one would expect from Barnes, this is a book not just of actions, or of images, but of ideas. There is much reflection, most of it sane, about the nature of love and jealousy, Graham wondering why jealousy exists, why it happens to him, and whether (since it has happened to him for no reason he can identify, and analysis cannot reduce it) perhaps it means that love inevitably goes wrong. In Graham's thinking about Jack's novels, especially his use of real people, slightly disguised, as characters, are the beginnings of the investigation of the relations between art and life that will be so central to *Flaubert's Parrot* (there is much about France here, as in *Metroland,* and recondite pieces of French medieval history too).

At a deeper level Barnes is working out ways of illustrating an idea about humanity. His novel has two epigraphs: the shorter, from Moliére, admits that *"Il vaut mieux encore être marié qu'étre mort"* (it is better to be married than to be dead); while the second, from a journal of psychology, has to do with the human being's "three brains," the oldest of which is the reptilian, beneath or beyond civil control. The third or "highest" brain, "a late mammalian development," is relatively powerless. Jack Lupton knows the same theory, and tells Graham about the lower brains, which "control our emotions, make us kill people, fuck other people's wives, vote Tory, kick the dog" (74). Jack portrays the inside of the head as "one layer of Four-Eyes, two layers of Sawn-Offs" (75). The "Four-Eyes" are (metaphorically) bespectacled ninety-pound weaklings, civilized but ineffectual. The "Sawn-Offs" are so called, apparently, because they are the "lower" brains, the less evolved; irrational and stunted, they are amoral and frightening. Ann is not privy to this discussion, but she seems to be hinting at a similar theory when, trying to account for her growing dislike for Graham, especially after his fit of jealousy has ruined their dinner party, she thinks, "He'd reverted" (143).

The reptilian brain is clearly linked to important questions of freedom and determinism. Graham wonders if the theory means that "it's not our fault"; Jack counters with a hypothesis that most people are not under the control of their primitive brains:

> Most people don't kill other people. Most people have got the Sawn-Offs well under their thumb, I'd say. Most people control their emotions, don't they? It may not be easy, but they do. I mean, they control them enough, don't they, and that's what it's all about, that's what we're talking about. And without embarking on the neurology of it, I'd say that either the second eleven know which side their bread's buttered, or perhaps the prefects really know how to handle them. (76)

This reassuring account may seem less reassuring when Graham Hendrick—nice man, reasonable modern human being, intellectual, considerate lover—proves finally unable to keep his emotions under control and commits murder. The novel never attempts to answer the ultimate question of freedom and control, but it is there throughout; why Graham cannot escape his jealousy, why Jack is an habitual adulterer, why Ann occasionally wounds Graham by extra, untrue confessions of old affairs.

In an interview with Patrick McGrath, Barnes endorses the three-brains theory and goes on to give the following account of *Before She Met Me,* which illustrates the timelessness of Barnes's central concerns:

> In a way it's a sort of anti-'60s book. It's against the idea that somehow the 60s sorted sex out, that everyone was all fucked up beforehand. Queen Victoria was still in charge—and then along came the Beatles, suddenly everyone started sleeping with everyone else, and that cured the lot. That's a rough plan of English sexual history, as seen by many people. And I just wanted to say, it's not like that; that what is constant is the human heart and human passions. And the change in who does what with whom—that's a superficial change.[7]

CHAPTER FIVE

Flaubert's Parrot

Published in 1984, *Flaubert's Parrot* represented a major step forward in Julian Barnes's career. It was, as he has said, his breakthrough—widely reviewed, popular, the book that made him one of Britain's young novelists to watch. It has been described as "the tour de force that introduced him to American readers" and led to his first two books being published in the United States.[1] Moreover, it inaugurated the ongoing controversy over whether the books Barnes writes are novels or something else—a controversy which, naturally enough, quieted down with his very different next novel, *Staring at the Sun,* but reignited with *A History of the World in 10½ Chapters.*[2] A book about Flaubert's parrot? One in which one chapter is a bestiary, another an examination paper? A novel which includes something called "The Train-spotter's Guide to Flaubert"? What sort of novel is this?

To start with, it really is about Flaubert's parrot. The book begins and ends with the efforts of the narrator, Geoffrey Braithwaite, to discover what has happened to a parrot Flaubert possessed while he was writing the story "Un coeur simple." On a trip to France in search of Flaubert scenes and memorabilia, Braithwaite comes across a stuffed parrot in a museum, alleged to be the parrot in question; unfortunately he soon sees another one for whom the same claim is made.[3] By the end of the novel, the two birds have multiplied into a roomful of birds, and certainty on this particular question seems ever further away.

Barnes often writes, or writes about, alternate versions. Here are two alternate parrots, with nothing to dictate a choice between them. Pursuing the search does not reduce the alternatives but increases them. It is emblematic of the difficulty of knowing the truth, and a Flaubertian irony: in this sense the inconclusive pursuit of Flaubert's parrot is both a believable activity for a man devoted to Flaubert and a symbol for the book.

In a broader sense this is a book about Flaubert, as some of the chapters—for instance, taxonomies and enumerations of the role of trains in Flaubert's life, or the presence of various animals in his life and work—make clear. And the meaning of Flaubert's parrot ramifies further and deeper, becoming a complicated and subtle examination of truth, knowledge, art, and love. But all this is obliquely approached through the parrot and related questions about Flaubert's biography.

Flaubert's Parrot is certainly different from the first two Barnes novels and the Duffy books. One mark of difference is the narrator. In *Metroland* the story is told retrospectively by a narrator who is also the main character. It is *homodiegetic;* it uses, in the traditional terminology, "first-person narration," and the person who speaks in first person is the person the book is about. Christopher Lloyd tells us his story. He is self-conscious about being a narrator and occasionally addresses the reader, or at least speaks to "you": "How does adolescence come back most vividly to you?"[4] His discourse is straightforward, transmitting the story in much the same order in which it happened, though large chunks are naturally left out. *Before She Met Me* has a different narrative procedure (as is—usually—required for a book in which the main character kills himself). Here the narrator is a

knowing entity, not a character in the book: what is convention-
ally called a third-person omniscient narrator. It is important that
the reader share the consciousness of Graham, Ann, and Jack, and
this method, which gives deep authoritative explanations of what
all of them, not just Graham, think and feel, permits it.

The Duffy books are narrated by a different kind of
heterodiegetic, or "third-person," narrator—that is, one whose
point of view is closely tied to that of Duffy. The reader knows
what Duffy knows, though the discourse of the narrator is more
fluent and vivid than Duffy's own language. While the reader is
confined to what Duffy sees, it is not Duffy who says it. The
narrative is focalized in Duffy, vocalized by another. This is,
once again, the most practical narrative stance for mystery and
detective novels, in which the suppression and withholding of
information are important parts of the desired effect.

For *Flaubert's Parrot* Barnes has devised a different kind of
narrator entirely: Geoffrey Braithwaite, retired physician with an
intent, though amateur, fascination with Flaubert, what he calls
his "rash devotion to a dead foreigner."[5] Aside from the Flaubert
interest, which his creator obviously shares, Geoffrey is very
different from Julian Barnes. As Braithwaite says: "I thought of
writing books myself once. I had the ideas; I even made notes. But
I was a doctor, married with children. You can only do one thing
well: Flaubert knew that. Being a doctor was what I did well. My
wife . . . died" (13). He is writing a book now, of course, but not
without misgivings and hesitations, as he explains:

> I hope you don't think I'm being enigmatic, by the way. If
> I'm irritating, it's probably because I'm embarrassed; I told

you I don't like the full face. But I really am trying to make things easier for you. Mystification is simple; clarity is the hardest thing of all. (102)

The small amount of information he wants to share about himself is, at least initially, superficial:

I've got brown eyes; make of that what you will. Six foot one; grey hair; good health. But what matters about me? Only what I know, what I believe, what I can tell you. Nothing much about my character matters. No, that's not true. I'm honest, I'd better tell you that. (96)

Despite his modesty, despite his contempt for critics, Braithwaite has decided views on many matters beyond (though connected with) Flaubert, including the relations between literary form and content or the function of the novel; at one point he plays a game of being a literary dictator, forbidding ten different categories of novel, including those about incest, those about God, those in which the narrator or a character is identified only by an initial, those set in Oxford or Cambridge, and so on.

In every fiction with a homodiegetic, or "first-person," narrator, no matter how self-effacing, transparent, or unimportant he or she aspires to be, that narrator is an important subject of the novel. The alert reader realizes that the narrator's way of seeing things and his way of presenting them (shaping, withholding, decorating, arranging) are, even if not in any way dishonest, nevertheless human, partisan, and refracting. Every such narrator is in some sense "unreliable": the communication of "truth" is always affected by the character, needs, and psychology of the person communicating it, and eventually the medium becomes the subject of the reader's interest. Famous illustrations of this truth include Nelly Dean in *Wuthering Heights,* the governess in *The Turn of the Screw,* and Nick Carraway in *The Great Gatsby.* No narrator is really "just passing along the facts." Geoffrey Braithwaite is no exception—as he well knows. He explains:

> Three stories contend within me. One about Flaubert, one about Ellen [his wife], one about myself. My own is the simplest of the three. . . . My wife's is more complicated, and more urgent; yet I resist that too. . . . Books are not life, however much we might prefer it if they were. Ellen's is a true story; perhaps it is even the reason why I am telling you Flaubert's story instead. (85–86)

Geoffrey Braithwaite is more candid than most narrators about his needs. By his own account a "hesitating narrator" (90), he begins to tell about his wife: "I remember . . . but I'll keep that for another time" (76). So he tells Flaubert's story to avoid telling his own and Ellen's (though eventually these stories come out). Barnes has another need; his technique is more complex. He has no need to use Flaubert's story as a way of avoiding Braithwaite's; he uses Braithwaite's telling of Flaubert's story as Braithwaite's way of telling his own story, mostly against his will and without his knowledge. Moreover, the two stories are not so much alternatives as they are echoes or foils for each other. Barnes

juxtaposes Flaubert's story with Braithwaite's because of interesting parallels and resonances between them. Terrence Rafferty
comments on the artfulness of this selection:

> Barnes has made him [Braithwaite] smart and funny and
> perfectly self-aware (he even acknowledges our suspicion
> that he murdered his wife). . . . Too much correspondence
> between the narrator's Flaubert research and his summing
> up of his own life, and the novel would be just another over-
> determined literary stunt, a donnish tour de force . . . too
> little, and the conceit is pointless—or pointlessly arbitrary,
> which might be worse.[6]

For a narrator, Geoffrey Braithwaite is unusual because he
does so little narrating, that is, telling a story. There is the small
and inconclusive story about his researches into the whereabouts
of Flaubert's parrot; there is the larger matter of Flaubert's life,
his significance, but the way this appears here is hardly a
narrative, and what Braithwaite does with it is hardly telling a
story; there is, finally, the story of himself, his wife, and his
marriage, which comes out in fugitive asides and hints until,
finally, in a chapter called "Pure Story," he gives us its outline,
though even here much remains vague or ambiguous. David
Leon Higdon accurately characterizes this as:

> a most oblique and reluctant confession by a man who
> blames his hesitation on his typically reticent English
> nature, on his own embarrassment, and finally on his fear
> of unmasking himself as a cuckold, especially after he has

earned the reader's respect by way of his erudition, his sincere love of Flaubert and his skilful amateur sleuthing.[7]

Instead of narrative, Braithwaite provides an impressive mix of other types of prose; as Higdon argues, relating this book to James Joyce's *Ulysses* and D. M. Thomas's *The White Hotel:*

> *Flaubert's Parrot* deftly deconstructs itself into various types of competing documents: the chronology, biography, autobiography, bestiary, philosophical dialogue, critical essay, manifesto, "train-spotter's guide," appendix, dictionary, "pure story" and even examination paper.[8]

Chapter 8, "The Train-spotter's Guide to Flaubert," illustrates well the complex and witty workings of this novel. British train-spotters are hobbyists who spend their spare time on station platforms recording the identifying numbers of locomotives in an attempt to spot them all. The hobby is usually derided as ineffably boring, appealing only to cranks and misfits, often teenaged boys. For Braithwaite to identify himself as a train-spotter shows some ironic distance from his devotion to a dead foreigner. Still, the chapter enumerates appearances of trains in the author's life and books, concluding with a train Braithwaite spotted going by Flaubert's house, complete with his reflection on its likely (ironic) contents (poisons, enema pumps, and cream tarts). The chapter title ironizes and undercuts the contents, but they do not remain undercut. The title invites the reader to take Braithwaite at his most self-deprecating estimate—a harmless obsessive making a pointless count—but like his other gestures of self-protective self-mockery, this one is temporary.

To explain why this book contains a train-spotter's guide at all, or an exam paper or a bestiary, James B. Scott has recourse to the same explanation as Higdon—the postmodern theory of deconstruction—when he says that the "medley of prose genres . . . deconstructs the conventional distinctions between fiction and non-fiction" and that the structure achieves "a deconstruction of prose genre taxonomies as a means of signification; the reader is at all times caught between the poles of true and not true, so that even the conventional signification patterns (biography presents fact; fiction presents fancy) no longer function."[9]

There is a less theoretical explanation, as well, for the diversity of nonnarrative kinds of prose discourse in this book. Geoffrey Braithwaite has already expressed his unwillingness to write books, claiming the one thing he can do well is the practice of medicine. Moreover, the book he has actually produced has an impromptu quality. For instance, he comments, "I'd ban coincidences, if I were a dictator of fiction" (67). By the next chapter but one he *has* become a dictator of fiction, playfully legislating against novels set in South America, novels including sex in the shower, and so on. Reflecting on irony, in chapter 7, "tempts me to write a Dictionary of Accepted Ideas about Gustave himself" (87); in chapter 9 he tells the reader that it is coming along well; and, sure enough, that is what chapter 12 is. Chapter 10, "The Case Against," includes the charge that Flaubert was beastly to women; reflecting on Louise Colet, the mistress whom Flaubert treated badly, Braithwaite thinks, "Perhaps someone should write her account: yes, why not reconstruct Louise Colet's Version? I might do that. Yes, I will" (135); and chapter 11 *is* Louise Colet's Version, written not just with sympathy to her claims and needs but in her voice.[10]

It is easy to see, then, how sharply the nature of the narrator and the nature of the narrative distinguish this book sharply from Barnes's fiction up to 1984. This point need not be stressed too forcefully, though, as there are important areas of continuity as well. Among them are France, Flaubert, and fidelity.

Barnes has always obviously been "an English Francophile,"[11] and this love stands out in Christopher Lloyd's adolescent fantasies about and then residence in France, as in Graham Hendrick's relatively idyllic holiday in the south of France with Ann (one of the areas left available by Ann's previous trips with previous men); here is a book entirely about France, set in France, except when it delves lovingly into the details of an Englishman's going to and coming back from France. The country, and especially the relationship of English people to the land and the culture, have remained among the constants of Barnes's work, including his own autobiographical essays, his book of short fiction, and most of his novels.

A second area of continuity concerns Flaubert. Barnes often quotes Flaubert's bon mot about prose being like hair, which shines from combing. He has become something of a Flaubert expert, as shown in a 1991 appearance at the Hay-on-Wye literary festival with Mario Vargas Llosa, the Peruvian novelist who has also written a book about Flaubert, *The Perpetual Orgy.* Andrew Billen's account of the occasion asserts that "*Flaubert's*

Parrot is now not so very much less well known, even in France, than Flaubert's Bovary"; and, comparing Barnes's talk to a courtship of Emma Bovary, Billen says that

> If close textual knowledge and adroit jokes . . . are paths to a fictional lady's heart, Barnes, dressed in charcoal-grey jacket and open-necked white shirt, would win Emma's hand. Expansive with his hand gesture and pronouncing words like "Flaubertine" and "Flaubertian" in a perfect French accent, he has worked out the timetable of the novel's carriage scene and estimates that it adds up to "four or five hours of sex in a cab."[12]

This sounds a bit like Geoffrey Braithwaite, in fact, who has also studied the famous sex-in-a-cab section of *Madame Bovary* as well as an 1855 travel book about Normandy by an English clergyman and discovered that Rouen cabs were tiny and cramped and even less promising places for four hours of sex than readers might ordinarily imagine.

Barnes's admiration for Flaubert is a tribute from one writer to another. He comments in an interview:

> Obviously, he's the writer whose words I most carefully tend to weigh, who I think has spoken the most truth about writing. And it's odd to have a foreign genius for whom you feel a direct love. . . . He's obviously a tricky bastard in some ways, but I find when I'm reading his letters I just want to go and make him a cup of hot chocolate, light his cigarette.[13]

FLAUBERT'S PARROT

Higdon has cleverly, though perhaps not persuasively, traced Flaubert through Barnes's novels: in *Metroland,* he argues, the first section takes as its Flaubert text the *Dictionaire des Idées Reéues;* in section 2, Christopher's Parisian experiences, "Flaubert's *L'Education Sentimentale* is the intertextual authority"[14]; the third section, in which Christopher discovers his cuckoldry, presumably links with *Madame Bovary,* as *Before She Met Me* does, with its protagonist's overt and violent obsessions with his wife's adultery, and (of course) *Flaubert's Parrot,* where the narrator must acknowledge his wife's real, continuous, and apparently insatiable infidelity.

His apparently dispassionate avowal of Ellen's betrayals, though the dispassion is belied by both his evasiveness and his own acknowledgment of his pain, suggests one reason for his interest in Flaubert: the author's supposed objectivity. This is more problematic than it seems: Flaubert aimed at objectivity, in some sense of the word, but clearly his passions and hatreds were always engaged both in life and in his art. Still, if objectivity means an ability to avoid caring too much, then Braithwaite would wish to have it; Flaubert, as his letters amply demonstrate, was always able to put his art before his love; his correspondence with Louise Colet, his mistress, is almost one long explanation of why his work prevents him from seeing her.

A similar displacement helps to explain Braithwaite's devotion to Flaubert: his "work," his research, his collecting and sorting of information (on, say, "the four principal encounters between the novelist and a member of the parrot family" [18]) are perhaps meant to provide an anodyne "objectivity" or at least to keep him busy, in a train-spotting way. This does not work, partly because his studies in Flaubert keep turning up parallels for his own situation, unlikely as these may seem. The obvious parallel with Emma Bovary he qualifies by clarifying that, unlike Emma, Ellen "wasn't corrupted; her spirit didn't coarsen; she never ran up bills" (164). But further, remembering a lecture by a critic of Flaubert, he says, "Look, writers aren't *perfect,* I want to cry, any more than husbands and wives are perfect. The only unfailing rule is, If they seem so, they can't be. I never thought my wife was perfect. I loved her, but I never deceived myself" (76). The story of Ellen is a running, usually completely implicit counterpoint to the story—or rather, not story but chronology, bestiary, alternate truth, dictionary of received ideas—of Flaubert.

The idea of fidelity further links *Flaubert's Parrot* with other Barnes fiction up to 1984. In its permutation of infidelity, or adultery, this is a familiar concern in Barnes's books. Perhaps not surprising, he is most often interested in the wife's infidelity to the husband, who (in *Metroland,* perhaps, in *Talking It Over,* in *Before She Met Me,* and apparently in *Flaubert's Parrot*) is, like Charles Bovary, more ordinary than his wife: not interesting enough or powerful enough to keep her love exclusively to himself. Charles Bovary, discovering the evidence of Emma's betrayal of him, concludes only that fate was to blame. Perhaps it is glib to define Barnes's interest in adultery and triangular relationships as part of his Francophilia, his way of incorporating this classically French fictional subject at the heart of his own English texts. Nevertheless the idea of fidelity, or of the possibility of fidelity, in marriage is crucial in almost all of Julian Barnes's novels.

FLAUBERT'S PARROT

But fidelity means more than not committing adultery. Braithwaite demonstrates a great deal of fidelity to Gustave Flaubert; Flaubert demonstrated fidelity to his art (often requiring infidelity to his mistress); and in this novel the most important examination of fidelity has to do with fidelity to fact or truth.

The reader has already seen Braithwaite's insistence that he is honest, that he tells the truth. But much of the book is devoted to the question of what truth is and how one can know it. This arises from the start in the question, surely somewhat absurd, of which is the real Flaubert's parrot? The parrot itself is of interest only because the novelist borrowed it to look at while writing about a fictional parrot in "Un Coeur Simple," so the search for "Flaubert's Parrot" is in part a question of the real-life original of a fictional character, in this case an animal. But there was a real parrot: where is it now? Braithwaite pursues this question, not very doggedly, and finds it incapable of solution. There are too many contradictions, too many competing versions of the truth, too many undecidable bits of evidence.

A related question—or rather series of questions, as all the variants of "fidelity to the facts" are canvased here—occurs in the chapter "Emma Bovary's Eyes," which is about factual "errors" in fiction. The starting point is a passage quoted from Dr. Enid Starkie, a famous academic critic of French literature, in which she claims that Flaubert was too careless to be consistent in giving the color of Emma's eyes, having them sometimes brown, sometimes deep black, and sometimes blue. Braithwaite reacts angrily in part because of the attack on Flaubert, toward whom he feels protective, and in part because of the presumption of critics condescending to creative writers (an objection shared by

Barnes[15]); but there is much more to it than this. Among his counterarguments, he points out that

—Enid Starkie, whom he once heard lecture at Oxford, "dressed like a matelot, walked like a scrum-half, and had an atrocious French accent" (79). This is pure ad hominem, except for the bad French accent; it is followed by the announcement that her book about Flaubert included a reproduction of an alleged painting of Flaubert that is in fact a painting of his friend Louis Bouilhet. So who is she to accuse him of making mistakes?

—Eye color doesn't matter much anyway. He points out that his wife Ellen's eyes were greeny-blue, which, according to the usual symbolism of eye color, would make her a combination of innocence and honesty (blue) and wildness and jealousy (green).

—"Factual mistakes" in imaginative literature don't matter very much. Here he quotes Christopher Ricks, who lectured on mistakes in *Lord of the Flies* and "The Charge of the Light Brigade." He distinguishes between external mistakes—for instance, about how many men were in the Light Brigade—and internal mistakes—for instance, about what color Emma's eyes were.

—But Flaubert does not in fact make the internal mistake of which Starkie accused him. Braithwaite assembles all the references to Emma's eyes in the novel and shows that they were brown but often looked black, or even blue, depending on changing light or Emma's mood.

—And furthermore, the woman on whom—according to Flaubert's close (but factually unreliable) friend Maxime du Camp—Emma was based had "eyes, of uncertain colour, green, grey, or blue, according to the light . . ." (81). This whole

FLAUBERT'S PARROT

argument is of great interest in relation to Barnes's theme of fidelity. Is internal consistency—fidelity to one's own imagined creation—important? Would it matter if Emma's eyes changed color in the course of the book? How about external consistency?—that is, may Emma's eye color in some way be explained by the eye color of her alleged "real-life original"? And must one believe Maxime du Camp's account of that woman's eyes, or even his declaration that she is the original of Emma Bovary? Other originals have been adduced for Emma, to say nothing of Flaubert's supposed claim, "Madame Bovary, c'est moi." But there is no agreement that Flaubert said this either.

But what about Enid Starkie and Christopher Ricks? These are real people. What are readers supposed to make of their presence in this work of fiction? Is Braithwaite telling the truth about them? Is Julian Barnes (who as a student of modern languages at Oxford is actually more likely than Geoffrey Braithwaite, even were he not a fictional character, to have heard Enid Starkie lecture)? Did Dr. Starkie have an atrocious French accent, and if it could be proven that her French was flawless, what impact, if any, would that have on a reading of *Flaubert's Parrot*? In 1984 Geoffrey Braithwaite was a living fictional person, Ellen Braithwaite a dead fictional person, Christopher Ricks a living "real" person, Enid Starkie (like Gustave Flaubert) a dead "real" person. In *Flaubert's Parrot* which of them is more *real*? How important is it to get their details right? Braithwaite finds out that Flaubert—traditionally seen, not least by himself, as some sort of towering giant—was six feet tall, and this discovery unsettles the six-foot-one Braithwaite. Were tall men shorter then?

UNDERSTANDING JULIAN BARNES

Though there are many important philosophical questions raised by *Flaubert's Parrot,* the central one is the epistemological question about fidelity raised here, the question of reference. The traditional view is that words refer to things, or, to be slightly more accurate perhaps, words stand for mental concepts, which in turn answer to things in the world. Postmodern thinkers have denied that language has this referential function, or ability. In *Flaubert's Parrot* Barnes or Braithwaite seems to share their skepticism. How can language refer to the world? How can books refer to the world? Can one ever know the truth? Is there a truth?

The importance of these questions indicates that *Flaubert's Parrot* is, unlike Barnes's work up to 1984, a postmodern novel. But what does this mean? In one way, to declare it a postmodern novel is to excuse it from the requirements, or expectations, or "rules" which help to define a conventional English novel. Richard Locke defines this one as "a performance on the high wire, risky business that combines convention and flaming idiosyncrasy in ways that again evoke the memory of Nabokov."[16] A postmodern novel, almost by definition, refuses to satisfy the expectations of readers accustomed to realist, or high modernist, fiction.[17]

But defining the term purely as liberation or self-granted exemption from conventions is little help. Postmodernism implies both a method and an underlying theory. David Lodge, a novelist-critic some of whose novels follow a postmodernist direction, defines postmodernist fiction as a kind of writing that "continues the modernist critique of traditional mimetic art, and shares the modernist commitment to innovation, but pursues these aims by methods of its own. It tries to go beyond modernism, or around it, or underneath it, and is often as critical of modernism as it is of antimodernism."[18] In explaining what these "methods of its own" are by which postmodernism "seeks to find formal alternatives to modernism as well as to anti-modernism,"[19] Lodge enumerates these: contradiction; permutation; discontinuity; randomness; excess; and what Lodge calls "short circuit"—that is, devices that erase or confuse the distinction between the text and the world.[20] All of these are plentifully available in *Flaubert's Parrot:* the structure, particularly the passage from one chapter to another, demonstrates apparent randomness, for instance. The three different chronologies of Flaubert's life in chapter 2, or the presence of "Louise Colet's Version," are exercises in contradiction—and, unlike more conventional novels in which contradiction exists but is later reconciled, these are unresolved contradictions. Permutation, or "alternate narrative lines," exists in the chapter called "The Flaubert Apocrypha," which is about the books Flaubert meant to write but never did, the lives he meant to live but did not. Undoubtedly there is something excessive about, for instance, "The Flaubert Bestiary," which catalogs all references to animals in the author's biography, letters, or works, or "The Train-Spotter's Guide to Flaubert," anatomizing occurrences of and references to trains.[21] And the "short circuit"—any of a group of possible effects that confuse or eliminate the distinction between the text and the world, between fiction and life—is central to the novel. The whole book is about the connections, if any, between a story and the life to which it arguably refers.

Braithwaite is dubious about the possibility of knowing the truth. He says, "I'm not sure what I believe about the past"; he develops a metaphor for its unrecoverability: "the past is a distant, receding coastline, and we are all in the same boat," with a set of telescopes along the rail (of a cross-channel steamer), one of which at any given time will appear to bring the coastline into the "correct" focus: "But this is an illusion . . ." (91; 101). There are plenty of reasons for his doubt. Inability to settle minor questions about parrots, or major ones about Flaubert's nature, or, even closer to home, questions about Ellen Braithwaite make a skepticism about the possibilities of knowledge attractive.

Does the novel, then, suggest or manifest the complete unavailability of truth? This is what some readers have made of it. John Bayley disapproves of the "modish notions" he believes the book expresses:

> The conscious implication of *Flaubert's Parrot* is that since we cannot know everything about the past we cannot know anything; but its actual effect—and its success—is to suggest something different: that the relative confirms the idea of truth instead of dissipating it, that the difficulty of finding out how things were does not disprove those things but authenticates them. It may be that few things happened as they are supposed to, and many things did not happen at all, but why should this be a reason for abandoning traditional conceptions of history, of art, of human character?[22]

Bayley's interpretation demonstrates the problem he is trying to describe: the fugitive quality of certitude. Can a reader know with certainty that the book's "conscious implication" (in whose consciousness is this implication lodged?) endorses the modish notion that we cannot know anything? Is it possible to conclude that Barnes consciously intended to imply a fashionable skepticism but (accidentally?) produced a different effect? It is more likely that the effect Bayley celebrates is not Barnes's unwitting or undesired outcome but his own deeper theory. That the novel produces an effect on a reader that is at odds with the epistemological theories sometimes entertained by its protagonist implies no necessary self-contradiction on the part of the author. One explanation for Bayley's reading is that the past fifteen or twenty years in the English-language novel have seen the doctrine that "we cannot know anything" about the past become a very modish notion indeed. Its modishness will guarantee that, as readers may see by following the critical reception of Barnes's novels, it is regularly identified as Barnes's major theme. But Barnes's position is more tentative or more ambiguous than the postmodern skepticism about referentiality and knowledge.

Another critic of Barnes who does agree, more or less, with Bayley on the philosophical foundation of the novel receives it with approval. In a discussion of postmodernism that is specifically focused on *Flaubert's Parrot,* James B. Scott explains the assumptions that he believes underlie postmodern literary theory:

> reality and truth are the illusions produced when systems of discourse (especially artistic discourse) impinge on human consciousness. In practice, this has led postmodern novelists to strive to undermine hermeneutic responses to art by foregrounding the discourse that informs their artifact, thereby implying that not only is the final "meaning" of a work of art forever unknowable, but also *any* orthodox truth is actually a discourse-generated fluke.[23]

Scott argues, for instance, that it is impossible to know that Ellen Braithwaite committed suicide, despite such strong indications as her husband's statement that she was unable to face despair and that "She chose the exact dosage: the only occasion when being a doctor's wife seemed to help her" (181). The absolution that skepticism about such an important and (to those involved) painful point gives may explain why Geoffrey Braithwaite sometimes finds himself attracted to the position John Bayley considers the novel to be endorsing: "We can study files for decades, but every so often we are tempted to throw up our hands and declare that history is merely another literary genre: the past is autobiographical fiction pretending to be a parliamentary report" (90). But note that even the temptation to believe this only happens, for him, "every so often." In fact this is not a bad summary of the postmodern account of history as another fiction, another text, made "unreadable" or "indecidable" by its reliance (like that of all texts) on tropes or figures of speech; thus, the theory claims, history is unreliable as an index of what "actually" happened in "real life," whatever that may be. Postmodern theory insists that this is always and inevitably the case; Geoffrey Braithwaite admits that he is tempted to believe it every so often. Given the painfulness of his past, the temptation is not surprising.

Geoffrey Braithwaite and Julian Barnes stop well short of radical skepticism about the past—not to mention the wider skepticism about reality and truth reported by James Scott. Braithwaite doubts the possibility of finding out which was the "real" Flaubert's parrot, but this does not lead him to conclude that there was no real parrot; he disclaims the ability to explain his wife's life but never the reality of it.

FLAUBERT'S PARROT

"Chronology" wittily exploits the different ways of reading the past, in three alternate versions as the Flaubert chronology. The third is composed of quotations from the author. The first two, though, cover the same ground but with first a positive, second a negative approach. In the first chronology the entry for 1851–57 begins: "The writing, publication, trial and triumphant acquittal of *Madame Bovary*. A *succés de scandale,* praised by authors as diverse as Lamartine, Sainte-Beuve and Baudelaire" (25). The same year in the second chronology begins quite differently: "*Madame Bovary*. The composition is painful—'Writing this book I am like a man playing the piano with lead balls attached to his knuckles'—and the prosecution frightening" (29). Even more striking is the disparity at the time of Flaubert's death. I: "1880: Full of honour, widely loved, and still working hard to the end, Gustave Flaubert dies at Croisset" (27). II: "1880: Impoverished, lonely and exhausted, Gustave Flaubert dies" (31). The same sort of perspectivism informs the later "Louise Colet's Version," which is, of course, much different from the version familiar by now to readers of Flaubert's letters to Colet.

And yet: how fundamental is the difficulty in knowing what happened? Is there any real doubt (either in this novel or outside it) that a man named Gustave Flaubert lived and died, or that he died (in whatever mood) in 1880? That *Madame Bovary* was published, prosecuted, and acquitted? That Louise Colet was Flaubert's mistress? A real skepticism about knowing the past would have prevented Geoffrey Braithwaite from wasting his time traveling to France or forming gloomy reflections regarding what he persists in believing is the house Flaubert lived in.

Truth is slippery, baffling, hard to discover; but there is still truth, as his correction of mistakes about the past, made by Flaubert or Enid Starkie, proves. There is a difference between the past and an autobiographical novel, a difference between books and life. Braithwaite concludes sadly: "Books are where things are explained to you; life is where things aren't" (168).[24]

It is no surprise that *Flaubert's Parrot* has been so celebrated; and it is no real injustice that despite the author's continuously impressive career after 1984 and the good novels that have followed it, it still seems Julian Barnes's masterpiece up to now. One reviewer called it "an extraordinarily artful mix of literary tomfoolery and high seriousness,"[25] and this is a rarer combination than it may seem. In a wise and appreciative review Terrence Rafferty wrote that

> *Flaubert's Parrot* is a minor classic, and one of the best criticism novels ever, because its critic/narrator has some dignity, because his choice of subject makes emotional sense and because the book has a lively, questioning spirit. ... Barnes, in his offhand way, performs a couple of literary marriages straight out of critics' dreams: he's written a modernist text with a nineteenth-century heart, a French novel with English lucidity and tact.[26]

Barnes likes to tell interviewers wryly that critics expected him to follow *Flaubert's Parrot* with "*Victor Hugo's Dachshund*" or "*Tolstoy's Dachshund*."[27] True to the example of Flaubert, who "never wrote the same book twice,"[28] he followed it with a novel different in almost every way.

CHAPTER SIX

Staring at the Sun

In 1986 Julian Barnes followed *Flaubert's Parrot* with *Staring at the Sun*. As his exasperated reactions to its critical reception (quoted in the previous chapter) make clear, it disappointed many reviewers, at least in England. The reasons for this reception are complicated; its effect on Barnes is slightly amusing. He has said about this novel, "As soon as you say you were disappointed, I get deeply protective about the novel. I say: Carlos Fuentes liked it—so sod you. This is the writer's response. It's like criticising your fourth child."[1] Indeed the distinguished Mexican novelist Fuentes, writing in *The New York Times Book Review* hailing this "brilliant new novel," saluted "the universal English voice of Julian Barnes, as he breaks barriers of conventional time and genre, creates characters from ideas and language, and stares not only at the sun but at the reader's intelligence."[2]

Mark Lawson's characterization of Julian Barnes as "like the teacher of your dreams: jokey, metaphorical across both popular and unpopular culture, epigrammatic"[3] applies nicely to *Flaubert's Parrot* but hardly at all to *Staring at the Sun,* which is his least witty book before *The Porcupine* and, because his protagonist is unintellectual, his least *overtly* brilliant.

Written in three sections, like *Metroland* and *Talking It Over,* this novel is the story of Jean Serjeant, a woman who is born in 1922 and lives a very long life (at the end of the book the year is 2021) without doing anything most people would consider important. She marries, leaves her husband after twenty years of marriage, bears one son, works at uninvolving jobs until retirement, and travels widely. Her reflections on her life rarely rise above the commonplace; in the third section her son, Gregory, assumes a more central place in the narrative, and he is more of a thinker—or at least worrier—than Jean, but he is also colorless.

The high points of Jean's life are, by the usual standards, very low. In her youth she goes golfing with a colorful but somewhat disreputable uncle, and these outings include minor cheating, screaming at the sky, and the "Shoelace Game," in which players untie their shoes and put their feet in them over the shoelaces, then pull them out for a ticklish frisson. In middle age she visits the Grand Canyon and experiences a sort of epiphany there. In old age, in fact at the very end of the novel, she goes up in an airplane and, because the pilot climbs rapidly, is able to see the sun setting twice. In between, Jean's marriage is indeed an unhappy one, but not in any sensational way; her husband, a limited man, hits her once, not painfully, in twenty years, when she suggests that their long failure to bear children might be his fault rather than hers. The narrator characterizes the marriage by comparing it with their unsatisfactory honeymoon as "the longer, slower dismay of living together" and "the slow dulling of enjoyment and the arrival of tired discourtesies."[4]

All these qualities of *Staring at the Sun* are, at least on first examination, unpromising. And this lack of apparent promise may have been part of the motivation for writing this novel. Barnes has spoken repeatedly about wanting to face challenges in his writing, as well as his desire to write something different each time out. His career has raised questions such as the one

STARING AT THE SUN

expressed by Mira Stout: "Is Julian Barnes a potentially great novelist with a restless streak, or is he a middling talent masking his shortcomings with formal trickery?"[5] It is possible to imagine that he decided to write *Staring at the Sun* without formal trickery partly to make questions like this one irrelevant. Barnes's own explanation is not quite this, but he does believe that the book is "underrated, in that it looks less adventurous than *Flaubert's Parrot,* but I think it took a fair amount of risks. . . . Some people who didn't like it wanted it to be more socially realistic. That wasn't what I was after."[6] English critics may have been disappointed by the novel's lack of social realism or obvious technical brilliance; in fact American reviews were typically positive: Fuentes, writing in *The New York Times Book Review,* was the most enthusiastic, but Ann Hulbert, in the *New Republic,* wrote that "[b]eneath the surface simplicity of the prose and the story, the novel conveys a sense of mystery more reminiscent of fable than of the cerebral fiction Barnes has written before"; Richard Eder invoked *Tristram Shandy, Brave New World,* and Flaubert's "A Simple Heart" (the one with the parrot) and called it a "pulsating fable"; Christopher Lehmann-Haupt, writing in the daily *New York Times,* hinted a wistful regret that the book lacked "extreme forms of narrative slight of hand" but ended by praising the "quieter game" it plays.[7] Mira Stout provides one of the most thorough celebrations:

"Staring at the Sun" . . . balances grand themes with gemlike wit. Arguably Barnes's strongest novel, the book takes its protagonist, Jean Sergeant [*sic*], a pliant, uneducated woman, from childhood to death with compassionate insight into her longings and disappointments, and celebrates the small miracles that sustain her.[8]

One more comment from Barnes is worth noting, though it complicates any understanding of the relationship between *Flaubert's Parrot* and *Staring at the Sun:*

> Well, the first thing to say is that I started *Staring at the Sun* before I started *Flaubert's Parrot;* I'd already written about 30,000 words of it. The connection that I see between the two is technical rather than thematic, in that *Flaubert's Parrot* is a book that went off in all directions, and one of the ways of tying it all together was to use repeated phrases and ideas like thin bits of gossamer, to keep it vaguely bound together. That developed in *Staring at the Sun* into actual images, and incidents, and stories, which, as the story continues, take on more depth and significance.[9]

Perhaps because it is not defensive, this is the author's most helpful comment on his novel.

If there is a thematic connection between the two novels, it has to do with love; Jean Serjeant is not an artist, nor is anyone else in this novel, and the philosophical treatment of how art and life are related is absent from this book; likewise adultery is absent, and sex is relatively unimportant. After her ex-husband is long dead, Jean considers a lesbian affair with Rachel, her son's lover, who invites her to spend the night, but decides against it (the kind of veering away from the sensational of which the plot

STARING AT THE SUN

is made up). Jean had learned to enjoy sex a little in marriage—it reminds her of the Shoelace Game—but soon comes to think of going to bed with her husband as "just part of running the house" (74). Nevertheless this novel is interested in love, though Jean has never had any happiness in romantic love. She loves her son, Gregory, and her relations with two men in her early life—Uncle Leslie, the golfer, and Sun-Up Prosser, the pilot who lived with her family in wartime—are the most important influences on her. Still, there is a tart impatience with men in this novel: it is outspoken and vehement from the feminist Rachel; with Jean it takes the form of reflections such as "She wondered why mosquitoes didn't give up on victims who had reached a certain age, and hunt for younger flesh instead; as men did" (95) or "being in China was like living with a man" (136).

Another thematic echo of *Flaubert's Parrot* reminds the reader of the last chapter of that book, in which Geoffrey Braithwaite specifically contrasts Flaubert with his own dead wife Ellen. Defending the novelist against the false claim that he had committed suicide, Braithwaite quotes Flaubert on the futility—and bad manners—of bellowing against Providence: "'People like us must have the religion of despair. By dint of saying 'That is so! That is so!' and gazing down into the black pit at one's feet, one remains calm.'"[10] Ellen Braithwaite, by contrast, was unable to gaze into the black pit, and, her husband implies, that is why she committed suicide.

"Staring at the sun" is an obvious analogue to gazing into the black pit. It begins as a real fact. Sergeant Thomas Prosser, a fighter pilot in World War II, sees the sun come up while flying back across the English Channel from a raid over France;

dropping his plane down sharply to look at a ship, he gets himself below daybreak and sees it rise again.

Prosser, nicknamed "Sun-Up" for this accomplishment and sidelined from the war because he has lost his nerve, is billeted with Jean Serjeant's family, where he tells her about his experiences in the skies. Talking to Jean about the best way of being killed, something he has thought about obsessively, he gives a very circumstantial account of flying up into the sun:

> You're climbing straight into the sun because you think that's safe. It's all much brighter than usual up there. You hold your hand up in front of your face and you open your fingers very slightly and squint through them. You carry on climbing. You stare through your fingers at the sun, and you notice that the nearer you get to it, the colder you feel. You ought to worry about this but you don't. You don't because you're happy. (31)

Happiness is delusive because, as he explains it, the happiness comes from an oxygen leak, and the next thing that happens is that, one way or another, you die; and Prosser says, "I can see myself doing that one day" (32). When, long after the war, Jean traces Prosser's widow and asks for an account of his death, she learns that he was last seen climbing straight into the sun, one hand before his eyes, then dropping into a fatal dive.

Courage and the lack of it are important concerns of this novel. Sun-Up Prosser has lost his nerves, "got the wind up." Uncle Leslie, the charmer of Jean's childhood, is thought to have succumbed to cowardice, since he left England for the United

States just after the Munich agreement, to return only after the war was over; on his deathbed he confesses, "I was never brave" (130), even though he is facing cancer bravely. Jean is afraid of her wedding night, afraid of being inadequate, and her courage is tested by twenty years of marriage to an insensitive husband, then by her willingness to leave him, becoming independent, just when she has given birth at age forty. Gregory is afraid of death. Jean is the truly courageous person in this novel, though, as a woman, she has fewer opportunities to display bravery. Courage is usually defined as willingness to do the kinds of things men do:

> We do tend to think of courage as a male virtue, as something that happens in war, something that consists of standing and fighting. But there are 85,000 other sorts of courage, some of which come into the book—banal forms of courage—to live alone, for example, social courage. Then, the sort of sexual courage that we see in the relationship of the two women, Jean and Rachel.[11]

Gregory wonders if it is brave to believe in God, and it is mostly in Gregory that this book's strong theological element is found. Jean has no faith and no need for any. Julian Barnes is himself without religious belief, having—at the time he wrote this book—never been to church. He summed up his own theological position for Kate Saunders: "There is either a God and a plan and it's all comprehensible, or it's all hazard and chaos, with occasional small pieces of progress. Which is what I think."[12] But this rather breezy statement of agnosticism, along with the claim that there are only two positions, badly belies the theological sophistication of *Staring at the Sun* (and its successor, *A History of the World in 10½ Chapters;* Julian Barnes clearly becomes more interested in spiritual matters in his novels of the late 1980s). In the same interview with Saunders, he decries "man's need for God," implying, as much of the novel does, that God is a defense men turn to because they are afraid: God is the hand we put before our eyes because we cannot stare directly at the sun.

Gregory systematically explores what he considers to be all the hypotheses about divinity—many more than the two simple oppositions Barnes acknowledges for himself: either there is a God and a plan; or there is no God and only randomness occasionally punctuated by progress—making a list of fourteen possibilities, including the existence of God and the nonexistence of God and going on to the theory that God did exist, does not now, but will again; the theory that God exists only as long as people believe in him; and the theory that there are several Gods, whose failure to act like God (by reducing human misery, for instance) is explained by too much democracy or by powerlessness. Though this list is presented with a certain amount of facetiousness—suggesting that the benign but powerless gods can only look on "like eunuchs in a harem" (165)—it is a serious set of propositions. Gregory takes it seriously.

His primary activity in old age (when Jean is one hundred he is sixty) is fearing death and asking questions. Since this is now the year 2021, he is able to put his questions to a supercomputer called GPC, the General Purposes Computer, which, beginning in 1998, put all human knowledge on-line. It has an even more

STARING AT THE SUN

specialized function, called TAT for The Absolute Truth, which Gregory consults for answers to his metaphysical questions. (The novel implies that the answers are actually supplied by human operators rather than the computer, though this may not be true of TAT.) From the computer he can get only data, when he needs much more, and irritating refusals to consider his inputs valid. So he asks Jean three questions: "Is death absolute?" "Is religion nonsense?" and "Is suicide permissible?" Her answers are "Yes, dear," "Yes, dear," and "No, dear" (187). The computer operators who, gossiping about Gregory after he logs off, have decided that he is a "stayer," and "being a stayer is a sort of bravery, don't you think?" (163) are talking about something else but getting around to the same point, the point made by Albert Camus in *The Myth of Sisyphus:* the crucial decision is whether to go on living; to do so, without the consolation of God—to look at the sun without a sheltering hand—is courage.

Gregory's questioning of the computer is part of a pattern of questioning that runs through the novel. Jean has always been a questioner. As a little girl she had a lot of questions, most of them derived from her reading or from Uncle Leslie's conversation:

as she grew up, she would find out the other answers. Answers to all sorts of questions. How to decide which club to use. Whether there was a sandwich museum. Why your Jews didn't enjoy golf. Whether her father had been frightened in the De Havilland, or just concentrating. How that Musso knew which way the paper folded. Why food looked quite different when it came out at the other end of

UNDERSTANDING JULIAN BARNES

your body. How to smoke a cigarette without the ash falling off. Whether Heaven was up the chimney, as she secretly suspected. And why the mink was excessively tenacious of life. (16)

She decides what she thinks about Heaven: it is a place in China, and very dusty; and she learns how to smoke a cigarette without the ash falling off (Uncle Leslie's trick, explained to her on his deathbed). Other questions are never answered. She asks Michael, her future husband, the one about the mink, and—hardly a surprise—he finds this a silly question. Things do not change much; eighty years later she persuades Gregory to ask GPC—the supposed repository of all human knowledge—why the mink is excessively tenacious of life, and the response is "NOT REAL QUESTION" (151). Jean thinks about this and decides that "real questions" are just questions to which the person being asked knows the answer. "The serious questions always remained unanswered" (153).

The question about smoking a cigarette is a key connection to Uncle Leslie, one of the two important men—the other being Sergeant Prosser—in Jean's life. Richard Eder calls them "two unlikely archangels."[13] Uncle Leslie introduces some mystery into Jean's humdrum childhood. Her earliest memory is of his giving her a pot of hyacinths to store away until spring; just the tips are showing through the soil. When the hyacinths never seem to bloom, or even grow, she digs down and discovers that they are inverted golf tees. Later he likes to take Jean golfing with him, which he calls "going down the Old Green Heaven" (10)—another earthly paradise, like the dusty Temple of Heaven she sees many years later in Peking, to substitute for the Heaven she used to imagine up the chimney; he does his cigarette trick, teaches her the Shoelace Game, and puzzles her with observations about Mussolini, Jews, and the future of aviation. Sometimes they flop down on the fairway and scream at the sky—which is fun, and defiant, and possibly a bit like staring at the sun. Uncle Leslie also pays for her first experience in the air, a one-hour flight in a De Havilland that is supposed to cure her whooping cough, and, much later, buys her a one-day round trip by Concorde to the Pyramids.[14]

Clearly Uncle Leslie is one of the people connected with the mysterious, or the numinous, or the uncanny; for this novel is not just about being ordinary, but about the extraordinary that lies beneath or beyond the ordinary; about the transfiguration of the mundane, about "ordinary miracles."[15] Uncle Leslie can do "magic tricks." Uncle Leslie is connected, as Sun-Up Prosser is in another way, with air travel, which is a form of transcendence in this book. Leslie also gives the young Gregory a toy airplane, starting him on the path of making model planes, though Gregory thinks flying them is too risky. Uncle Leslie raises tantalizing questions, some of which Jean is never able to answer.

Another element of transcendence in this novel is provided by the idea of "wonders." When, in middle age, Jean becomes a world traveler, she decides to visit the seven wonders of the world and does so, though she has to make some substitutions. But she also makes a list of the "seven private wonders of life." These are birth, being loved (not loving), disillusionment, marriage, giving birth, "the getting of wisdom" ("you were under anaesthetic during much of this process"), and dying (182).

For Jean the getting of wisdom has not been finding the answers to her questions but learning that some questions have no answers; religiously, her getting of wisdom (as the conversation with Gregory indicates) is a loss. At the Grand Canyon she has an epiphany:

> Perhaps the Canyon acted like a cathedral on religiously inclined tourists, and startlingly argued without words the power of God and the majesty of his works. Jean's response was the opposite. The Canyon stunned her into uncertainty. . . . It was said that one of the worst tragedies of the spirit was to be born with a religious sense into a world where belief was no longer possible. Was it an equal tragedy to be born without a religious sense into a world where belief *was* possible? (100)

It is somehow not surprising when her second look at the canyon involves flight: she looks down and sees an airplane flying there—that is, below the surface of the earth, a sort of miracle—and is stunned into further wondering.

The network of references to airplanes is one of the technical devices that make this novel a rich composition. Airplanes function in this novel somewhat the way ships will in *A History of the World in 10½ Chapters*. Strictly speaking, they are not needed to give the book coherence. After all, it is the life of one person—even if her son is increasingly prominent in the third futuristic section—beginning with the first thing she remembers and ending with an event of her hundredth year. Actually it begins with a two-page prologue, the anecdote of Sergeant Prosser's seeing the sun rise twice; and it ends with the flight during which Jean Serjeant watches the sun set twice. The plane flies over a deserted golf course, bringing memories of Uncle Leslie and screaming at the sky; Jean looks at the sun a bit, as the clouds make fingers in front of it; she comforts the crying Gregory and then, all clouds gone, looks steadily into the sun before the plane turns to its descent. Looking at the sun, this book has suggested before, is like looking at death, something people cannot do. But Jean does it here, and her thought about Gregory—"You were a mother until the day you died" (196)—makes this, symbolically at least, the end of her life.[16]

So this novel has a strong narrative structure, from the beginning of a life to its end. It is divided into three parts: roughly youth, middle age, and old age. Part 1 ends with Jean's honeymoon; part 2 polishes off the marriage quickly, turns to Jean's travels and the getting of wisdom, and ends with the death of Uncle Leslie and the middle-aged Gregory's reflections on it; part 3 is about an ancient woman and Gregory's unanswerable questions.

But in addition to narrative thrust and architectonics of structure, this novel is enriched and deepened and held together by "images, and incidents, and stories, which, as the book continues, take on more depth and significance. At first they're just odd stories, but by the end they become metaphors."[17] This is the author's own explanation, and a good one. Some of the stories, it must be said, work better than others; some of the images have more resonance than others.

UNDERSTANDING JULIAN BARNES

Jean's question about the mink's tenacity of life is one of the leitmotifs of the book. As a girl she has a picture in her room showing mink trapping, underneath which is a text explaining mink trapping and including the phrase "The Mink is excessively tenacious of life . . ." (17). Jean does not understand what this means; it falls into a large group of other things she does not understand, many of them taken from Uncle Leslie's elliptical conversation about Jews or "Musso" (Mussolini), or his jokes. He tells Jean, for instance, that when Lindbergh flew the Atlantic he took five sandwiches with him but only ate one and a half; Jean, missing the point, asks where the others went, and Leslie, "irritated," tells her, "They're probably in a sandwich museum" (14). As she grows older she presumably learns to answer some questions, such as the one about a sandwich museum (though it must be said that she never develops any evident sense of humor), and forgets others, for instance, one about Mussolini. But she persists in asking why the mink is excessively tenacious of life. Late in life she asks Gregory to ask the computer; earlier, still naive but no longer a little girl, she is talking to her fiancée:

> He moved forward slightly as if preparing to kiss her, but she persevered. It was only one of childhood's questions, but she distantly felt that they ought all to be settled before her adult life began. "Why is the mink tenacious of life?" (37)

Michael is usually too slow and literal for Jean. But it is possible for a reader to understand why he is baffled and slightly irritated. Though the question of the mink's tenacity of life clearly has some symbolic connection with Gregory's speculations about death and suicide and Jean's own longevity, which shows that she is tenacious of life even if not excessively so, it still seems contrived. The futuristic part 3, which also enables Barnes to introduce some satire on the politics of aging, seems mainly designed to permit the introduction of GPC and TAT and thus some demonstration that some questions are beyond the reach of any source of answers, though the suggestion that they are not really supercomputers but young women dutifully feeding back answers undercuts this purpose.

The most successful images raised to metaphor are the related ones of flying and staring at the sun. The novel is pervaded by images of flying; it begins and ends with flight, and in between are not only Gregory's model planes and Jean's flights to the seven wonders but Gregory's mordant reflections on modern air travel and death, as well as Jean's vision at the Grand Canyon. Carlos Fuentes suggests the possibility that "Jean's airplane takes the place of a broomstick and she is a modern sorceress"; he reminds his readers that:

> like enchantment and disenchantment, planes rise and fall. Jean's myth is the myth of Icarus. Prosser one day climbs straight up into the sun and then crashes to his death. No matter; the exhilaration is perhaps worth it; the only way to enchant the world anew is to enchant its technology.[18]

Whether or not Fuentes carries conviction about Jean and Icarus, there is something ambivalent about flying, as Prosser's death and Gregory's speculations demonstrate; it can be scary—Gregory seems to fear it, and Jean's father was paralyzed with fear in the De Havilland, though he claims he was concentrating on getting her well, but it is exhilarating for Jean and Sergeant Prosser, a way of transcendence.

And staring at the sun is ambivalent, too. Prosser apparently dies from it. Even as he tells Jean about it he illustrates the combination of attraction and terror, the cold approach to the fiery sun, the desire to gaze on something it is not possible to look at directly. T. S. Eliot observed that mankind cannot stand too much reality. Human inability to stare into the sun without a screening hand is the inability to face the reality of our life which, this novel tries to show, is mundane, untouched with divine purpose, and closed by death.

And yet this ordinary life, this reality, has a spiritual side too. Jean at ninety-nine years old thinks:

> Of course we each had a soul, a miraculous core of individuality; it was just that putting "immortal" in front of the word made no sense. It was not a real answer. We had a mortal soul, a destructible soul, and that was perfectly all right. An afterlife? You might as well expect to see the sun rise twice in the same day. (192–93)

This passage is an emblematic one with which to typify *Staring at the Sun*. It follows Jean's reflection on a book she learned of in China on the destructibility of the soul. China is another of the leitmotifs of this book, the site where the destructibility of the soul, the disappointment of Heaven (it was dusty), unanswerable questions, the Gobi Desert (Uncle Leslie's term for a sand trap), a confusion between "Asian" and "ancient" (so that the aged Jean thinks of herself as an "Asian lady"), and an old Chinese greeting ("the sun has risen twice today") come together in a complex pattern of relationships. And of course Sun-Up Prosser *has* seen the sun rise twice in one day, so to compare the chances of an afterlife to seeing the sun rise twice in one day is (particularly for Jean, probably the only person who actually knows about Sun-Up Prosser's vision) an odd way of dismissing the possibility.

The passage shows Jean courageously staring at the sun: the destruction of the soul is "perfectly all right." And it shows that there are far more real questions than real answers. *Staring at the Sun,* like Jean Serjeant, is full of questions. That they are not answered hardly implies that they are not real questions; Barnes agrees with his heroine: "The serious questions always remained unanswered" (151).

CHAPTER SEVEN

A History of the World in 10½ Chapters

In a brief article based on an interview when *Staring at the Sun* was published in the United States, Barnes is quoted as saying that his next book will be "an American novel. Every English writer at some point thinks it's time to do his American one, with a twist no one else has tried."[1] One wonders what has happened to this book; perhaps it has joined the Julian Barnes apocrypha, comparable to the Flaubert apocrypha enumerated in chapter 9 of *Flaubert's Parrot,* along with the book about Oxford that was never published.[2] Whatever happened to the American book, the novel that actually appeared three years later was something very different.

If in *Staring at the Sun* Barnes had the courage to write a quiet book about an ordinary woman leading a relatively uneventful life, in his next book he had the courage to attempt something much more ambitious. Calling your book a history of the world, especially when it is only a little over three hundred pages long, is already a challenging gesture. Interpreting the title correctly has challenged Barnes's critics. Kate Saunders writes, surely with misplaced assurance, that *A History of the World in 10½ Chapters* is "just what the title promises—a fictional history of the world, or the gospel according to Julian Barnes."[3] Both Joyce Carol Oates and Robert Adams take the claim in the title seriously enough to contradict it, though with enough hedging to show that

A HISTORY OF THE WORLD IN 10½ CHAPTERS

they suspect the presence of irony; Oates, for instance, says that it "is neither the novel it is presented as being nor the breezy pop-history of the world its title suggests."[4]

Readers should notice that the claims of the title are less sweeping than first appears. For one thing it is not *the* history, but *a* history. No claim is made that this history is the right one; a reader soon discovers one of the major themes of the book, which is that there is no "the" history—there are only histories. Chapter 1 is a history of the Flood and Noah's ark told by a stowaway woodworm, and it is very different from "the" history as recorded (actually in two varying forms) in the Bible. History as "what happened" is attenuated to disappearance; history as "what somebody told about what happened" makes up the book. In French the same word, *histoire,* means both history and story, a point Barnes probably finds too obvious to make.

Moreover, the apparently grand claims of naming your book a history of the world are undercut by what follows: in 10½ chapters. A history of the world in 10 chapters would be odd enough, with the precision and the small number of chapters already implying an ironic twist; the half chapter makes the irony unmistakable. It provokes the reader to wonder what a half chapter is. Richard Locke recognizes the complicated effect of the title: the book's

comic grandiosity is apparent from its aggressive title. A history, then, not fiction; divided with confident precision into chapters, though we note the humorous, if whimsical precision of "10½." The title suggests a book that will flaunt genres, categories of communication, numbers that

don't neatly conform to our devotion to the order of ten.
This self-advertising title is a boast that mocks itself by
calling attention to its literary and cognitive form.[5]

Readers disappointed by the low-intensity "normality" of *Staring at the Sun* should have rejoiced at Barnes's return to flaunting
genres and heterogeneity of style and approach. Miranda Seymour
speaks for many, though, when she declares that "admirers of
Flaubert's Parrot are likely to feel a sneaking sense of disappointment with *10½ Chapters*."[6] Her problems with it put her in
the "'but-does-he-write-proper-novels' school of criticism,"[7] as
she says that "Biblical references and reappearing woodworm
don't provide enough logical connections to justify calling this a
novel, rather than a clever collection of linked stories of startlingly mixed quality."[8] Many other reviewers made the same
objection: Jonathan Coe flatly calls the contents "10 short stories"; while Joyce Carol Oates thinks it is "most usefully described as a gathering of prose pieces, some fiction, others rather
like essays."[9] D. J. Taylor writes that it "is not a novel, according
to the staider definitions; it possesses no character who rises
above the level of a cipher and no plot worth speaking of."[10] But
why should it conform to the "staider" definitions? Barnes has
been quoted previously on the definition of the novel he prefers:
"an extended piece of prose, largely fictional, which is planned
and executed as a whole piece."[11] Two parts of this definition
justify closer scrutiny: "largely fictional" and "planned and
executed as a whole piece." The first is a reminder that almost
every novel contains material that is not fictional, not just in the
trivial sense in which real people are renamed and introduced into

novels; no, almost every novel contains things that actually happened and places that actually existed. *War and Peace* places imaginary people at the (historical) Battle of Borodino; in *Northanger Abbey* the imaginary characters journey to the (historical) Bath; *Middlemarch* is importantly concerned with the (historical) coming of the railway to the (imaginary) town in which the story is set. Huckleberry Finn makes an imaginary journey down the historically recorded Mississippi River. Moreover, in *War and Peace* and *Vanity Fair* the fighting is precipitated by Napoleon Bonaparte, a real person. The introduction of historical figures in main roles, particularly controversial ones where they say and do things unsupported by the historical record, is a more recent development—in E. L. Doctorow's *Ragtime,* for instance, or Robert Coover's *The Public Burning,* which is *narrated* by Richard M. Nixon.

All this is well-known; less recognized, or at least less acknowledged, is that books of fact, including histories, are only "largely nonfictional," if that; fiction, or making, goes into every history or biography or autobiography, if only in the ordering of data, the selection of what to omit (which is, after all, almost everything), and the use of figurative tropes and interpretive metaphors. The woodworm tells of things that have been omitted from the biblical account of the Flood—including Noah's fourth son, hundreds of animals eaten by the human passengers (thus wiping out many species forever), Noah's unpleasant character and unhygienic habits, and the real role of the raven—and says that the length of the flood was much longer but shortened to forty days and forty nights for artistic reasons. "Fabulation," a recent term devised to describe postmodern approaches to fiction, appears in this novel, though as part of a psychiatrist's diagnosis of delusional activity: "the technical term is fabulation. You make up a story to cover the facts you don't know or can't accept. You keep a few true facts and spin a new story round them"[12] (109).

A History of the World in 10½ Chapters certainly is "largely fictional." One chapter is about Théodore Géricault's 1819 painting usually called "The Raft of the Medusa," and one is based on a trial of certain insects in fifteenth-century France; others rely on facts about the ill-fated ships the *Titanic* and the *St. Louis*. But most of the book is an imaginative creation by Julian Barnes. Deciding on the actual proportions would be difficult enough in any case, impossible in this, when one of the aims of the book is to unsettle the reader's confidence about the difference between truth and fiction, between history and story.

The second important part of Barnes's definition is the claim that a novel is "planned and executed as a whole." The planning is a matter known only to the novelist, and judging any work of art by its planning is inadvisable even when possible. Nor need "executed as a whole" mean in a continuous process, as many novels have issued from long, tortured, discontinuous, or confused writing processes.[13] What one is entitled to judge is whether the disparate parts of the novel are coherent and whether they appear to be a whole rather than collected stories or miscellaneous prose pieces. And some thoughtful readers of this novel have denied that it works as a whole. For them it is an anthology.

Clearly a novel like this makes greater demands on the author's unifying powers than one like *Metroland* or *Staring at the Sun*, each of which is held together by a central character and by a predominantly biographical pattern. After all, this is a book that begins with the woodworm's story of Noah and the Flood, which is followed by: the story of a cruise ship hijacked in the Mediterranean, evidently in the 1980s; the transcript of a fifteenth-century ecclesiastical trial of woodworms who damaged a bishop's throne and caused him injury; the story of a woman who may, apparently in the near future, have survived a nuclear war; the story of the wreck of the *Medusa,* in 1816, and a scholarly analysis of Géricault's painting of it; the story of a Victorian Irishwoman's attempt to scale Mt. Ararat; "three simple stories," essentially nonfiction, about the *Titanic,* the *St. Louis,* and a man swallowed by a whale; an account of a narcissistic actor making a movie in South America; another attempt at Mt. Ararat, this one featuring an American astronaut; and a dream of an afterlife. The "half" chapter, called "Parenthesis," is an apparently straightforward discussion of love spoken to the reader by Julian Barnes.

There is no main character, no unitary voice, no tight progression in the narrative, no single or even double plot. There is, it is true, a loosely chronological progression, in that the first chapter retells the most remote events, those connected with the Flood, and the last chapter is about Heaven. In between, though, chronological order is jumbled.

Moreover, the novel seems to be trying to exhibit a history of narrative in 10½ chapters. There are homodiegetic narratives told by narrators carefully created and distinguished from Julian Barnes, most obviously the woodworm of chapter 1, who tells his story retrospectively and with a reader-friendly, eager to persuade rhetoric. Kath, the "survivor" of chapter 4, tells part of her story in a present-tense style cognate with the diary, but it is spoken or thought rather than written; her account is framed and interspersed with another, delivered by an impersonal narrator; the two are inconsistent, and it is impossible to decide what the truth is. "The Visitors," chapter 2, is narrated by an impersonal, heterodiegetic narrator whose narrative is nonetheless tightly focalized in the main character, Franklin Hughes. The "history" in "Three Simple Stories" and "The Shipwreck" and the art history in the latter emanate from a knowledgeable speaker, the voice of nonfiction, though with a sense of humor unusual in history. "The Dream" is narrated in past tense, first-person by a man not, apparently, very different in some ways from what is known of Julian Barnes. "The Mountain" and "Project Ararat" are the most conventional narratives, given in a social-realistic style with an omniscient narrator. "Upstream" contains a single voice and is epistolary; because it is written as a series of letters and telegrams it has the same quality as "The Survivor" in Kath's reports: presentness, writing to the moment. "The Wars of Religion" is the transcript of a trial, and "Parenthesis" is no narrative at all but a sort of essay on love.

The novel is the most heterogeneous of the genres and is made up of all the kinds of material Barnes incorporates here. Even essays, such as "Parenthesis," appear frequently in classic novels. Still, Barnes's heterogeneity, by separating those elements that are usually blended and forfeiting chronological continuity and uniformity of narrating stance and voice, has created an extra challenge for him if this book is to seem unified. Richard Locke, though sympathetic to what the author is trying to do, does not believe it succeeds: "There are plenty of anecdotes ... but too few unifying actions or organically developing themes or arguments. The effect is not *collagiste* or symphonic: the presumably tragi-comic *concordia discors* remains discordant."[14] Naturally this judgment is arguable. In fact the novel does hold together; the disparate elements are sufficiently unified. Collage is not a helpful analogy, but symphony is. A musical composition has no plot and no characters and, in the usual sense, no ideas; instead it has themes and motifs, and the repetition and patterning of these provide its unity. *A History of the World in 10½ Chapters* has many repeated motifs as well. The first chapter introduces some of the most important of them, including

Woodworms and beetles. The narrator of chapter 1 is a woodworm. In chapter 3 woodworms are on trial. Woodworms are a threat to the letters sent out of the jungle in "Upstream!" Deathwatch beetles (*xestobium rufo-villosum*) are minor characters throughout; since the tapping they make is interpreted by human beings as some sort of signal of death, when in fact it is sexual behavior, they fit nicely into Barnes's speculations about love. There is a pair of them on the ark; in chapter 6, "The Mountain," Miss Ferguson compares the behavior of Turkish tribesmen near Mt. Ararat to the same insects.

The ark. Chapter 1 is all about Noah's ark (actually a small fleet); two later chapters are about modern attempts to find the ark; "Project Ararat" features a replica ark at Kitty Hawk, North Carolina, which is really a worship center; "Shipwreck" is partly concerned with why there have been so few paintings of the ark; the narrator of "The Dream" reveals that he met Noah in Heaven (though they could not communicate); Charlie, the self-obsessed actor in "Upstream," writes to his lover that he wants to move to the country and have a child: "I could make a playpen for him and buy him one of those big wooden Arks with all the animals . . . (206). The inhabitant of Heaven in the last chapter, among other pleasures, "ate more creatures than had ever sailed on Noah's Ark" (305).[15] "Trusting virgins," Julian Barnes explains in the "Parenthesis" on love,

> were told that love was the promised land, an ark on which two might escape the Flood. It may be an ark, but one on which anthropophagy is rife; an ark skippered by some crazy greybeard who beats you round the head with his gopher-wood stave, and might pitch you over-board at any moment. (229)

The literal arks have, obviously, shaded off into metaphorical arks, and there are many more of them. The "Survivor," who in a small sailboat has escaped what she believes is nuclear disaster, is accompanied by two cats, one male and one female: but "She didn't imagine some good-looking fellow turning up after a couple of weeks in a dinghy with two dogs on board; then a girl with two chickens, and a bloke with two pigs, and so on" (92). Stowaways: the woodworms and the deathwatch beetles are stowaways on the ark; this becomes an important legal argument in "The Wars of Religion": in "The Visitors" the Palestinian terrorists are also stowaways.

Voyages on other arklike vessels. These include the travels of the *Santa Euphemia* in "The Visitors," the *Medusa* in "Shipwreck," the *St. Louis* and the *Titanic* in "Three Simple Stories," Kath's sailboat in "The Survivor," and the Amazonian raft in "Upstream!"

Separation of the clean from the unclean. There is a good deal of discussion of this in the first chapter; the woodworm recognizes the irony that Noah's family favors the "clean" animals, bringing more of them on board the ark, but since they are considered edible (also, though Barnes does not make much of this, suitable for sacrificing to God) their "cleanness" is their doom. Noah and his family are horribly *unclean* by the animals' standards. After a nuclear accident in "The Survivor," officials separate contaminated animals from the "clean"; irradiated reindeer are marked off by a blue stripe on their carcasses as unfit for human consumption. In "The Visitors" the terrorists on the *Santa Euphemia* separate the passengers, with American Jews the least-favored group—i.e., the first to be killed—and other gradations moving down to the Irish and the Japanese, who appear to be the "clean" because their own countries have produced terrorists.

A similar sorting procedure is invoked in the third of the "Three Simple Stories," when it appears that some of the doomed Jews will be saved: "But how would you choose the 250 who were to be allowed off the Ark? Who would separate the clean from the unclean?" (184). The white Europeans rigidly separate themselves from the "unclean" South American natives in "Upstream," saying about the naked women, "Riddled with diseases I'm sure" (200). Charlie falls into a romantic sentimentalizing of the Indians, thinking them unable of deception or pretense—ethically "clean"—unlike the fallen Europeans. The troubles with the abandonment of the *Medusa* produced many forced separations, the most important being the separation of the officers from the enlisted men, who were briskly abandoned by the officers. When the *Titanic* was sinking, women and children were to be spared, men to die by drowning, though some men allegedly survived in women's clothing. The last chapter, which is about Heaven, includes a regret by the narrator that there apparently is no judging, no separating of the saved from the damned (Hitler is in Heaven). It seems a powerful human need to separate the clean from the unclean. Perhaps the distinction between fiction and nonfiction is akin to the separation of clean and unclean, and perhaps it is just as difficult to ascertain.

Gregory Salyer relates this process to the important issues of religion when he writes that "the sacred depends on difference and separation, clean and unclean, outside and inside. To be sanctified is to be set apart from the ordinary or evil forces of life."[16] This observation connects the clean/unclean distinction not only with the sacred/profane one but, by implication, with the normal/abnormal one. The account of the terrible wanderings of the *St. Louis* includes various deeply ironic uses of the word *normal,* echoed in "Upstream!," "The Survivor," and "The Dream."

These important patterns and repeated motifs hardly exhaust the ways in which Barnes has constructed the novel to show that, as Kath Ferris says, "Everything *is* connected, even the parts we don't like, especially the parts we don't like" (84). Reindeer are important repeated elements; Jews—modern Jews as victims in "The Visitors" and "Three Simple Stories," ancient Jews in the stories of Noah and Jonah; cannibalism; shipwreck; ships sailing around in circles; Jonah and the whale; even phrases, the repeti-

tion of which links one section to another. In "Upstream!"
Charlie uses the slang term "stinko-paralytico" for "drunk"; in
"The Dream" this appears as the name of a Yugoslav liquor.

That Julian Barnes can write ten chapters of disparate
material and then, by careful planning and executing, create links
to make these unified enough to be considered a whole rather than
ten parts does not necessarily justify the practice. The question
becomes: does this whole have some overall significance, some
thematic unity?

As one would naturally expect of Julian Barnes, always a
novelist of ideas, and especially in an ambitious book like this,
there are plenty of ideas. Probably the least compelling are those
about religion. Many reflective readers have realized that the
stories in the Bible are constructions made, at least in part, to
serve the needs of the people who had power to create them:
human beings (as opposed to reindeer or woodworms or ravens);
men; Hebrews. Any "blasphemy" found by readers of *A History*
will be more likely to arise in the facetiousness with which sacred
history is treated. The woodworm relates, breezily, that Noah was
a dirty, smelly drunk who was an incompetent navigator and
leader of men and that Ham's wife may have had a baby fathered
by an ape; and his reminder that everything Noah had was made
of gopher wood (his stave, his washbasin, his sandals) becomes
quite funny.[17]

But what Barnes is interested in is not religious belief but
religious history, which is part of his larger attention to history.
The two major themes of the book are history and love. The more
difficult proposition is that they are related: in some way love is

the remedy for history. Barnes has been quoted more that once saying roughly the same thing:

> I thought, what can we put up against the 24-wheeler that's bearing down on us all the time called history, with its little truck at the back called politics? The three main answers are religion, art and love. I think that religion isn't true, and art doesn't work for everyone. Love is the final fall-back position.[18]

What Barnes has to say, and to imply, about history is both clearer and more widely acceptable. It echoes Geoffrey Braithwaite's musing: "We can study files for decades, but every so often we are tempted to throw up our hands and declare that history is merely another literary genre: the past is autobiographical fiction pretending to be a parliamentary report."[19] If *A History of the World in 10½ Chapters* is a wholeheartedly postmodernist work, with the radical skepticism about knowledge, truth, and referentiality that implies, then Barnes shares Braithwaite's occasional pessimism. And, to be sure, the ten chapters demonstrate some of the shifty qualities of history. The woodworm's story of Noah suggests that history is the story told by the winners, implies that "our sacred history is but one story among many, one point of view among many points of view."[20] Kath Ferris, "The Survivor," is sure that she is the lone human survivor of a nuclear disaster, and the conversations she seems to be having with a doctor are figments of her imagination. The doctor is just as sure that Kath is delusional, that the nuclear disaster was averted, that she is suffering psychosomatic illnesses. Is her hair falling out because of nuclear illness (Kath's story, or history)? Or is she pulling it out (the doctor's story)? Did she reach an island where she and her two cats, one of them pregnant, started a new life? Or did she sail around the harbor in circles, fantasizing, until she and two starving cats were rescued? *It is impossible to know.* Similarly undecidable matters occupy the reader in most of the chapters. Salman Rushdie, reviewing *A History,* characterizes it as "the novel as footnote to history, as subversion of the given, as brilliant, elaborate doodle around the margins of what we know we think about what we think we know. This is fiction as critique. . . ."[21]

In the half chapter, "Parenthesis," Barnes comes as close as possible, for a novelist, to *speaking as himself,* without the distancing of narrator or implied author: he says it is himself and calls himself Julian Barnes. And there he argues:

> History isn't what happened. History is just what historians tell us. . . . One good story leads to another. . . . The history of the world? Just voices echoing in the dark; images that burn for a few centuries and then fade; stories, old stories that sometimes seem to overlap; strange links, impertinent connections. (240)

That is a provocative definition, which seems to be more and more about this novel itself as it accumulates. Nevertheless the novel seems insistent on demonstrating, as "Parenthesis" is insistent on declaring, the unreliability of history.

And that is probably, for most people at least, a depressing concept. In his half chapter, probably the most didactic piece of prose Julian Barnes has ever published, he suggests two responses to the unreliability of history. One is to act as if it is not true:

> We all know objective truth is not obtainable, that when some event occurs we shall have a multiplicity of subjective truths which we assess and then fabulate into history, into some God-eyed version of what "really" happened. . . . But while we know this, we must still believe that objective truth is obtainable; or we must believe that it is 99 per cent obtainable; or if we can't believe this we must believe that 43 per cent objective truth is better than 41 per cent. We must do so, because if we don't we're lost, we fall into beguiling relativity. . . . (243–44)

And the other response to the delusions of history is love. "Parenthesis" is mostly about love, a face-to-camera sort of confession of Barnes's own love and a celebration of its importance. While there is considerable debunking of popular myths—that love makes people happy, for instance—his endorsement of love is, finally, very powerful.[22] The love he recommends for "us"—i.e., human beings—is a demanding love: we must be precise about love; we must tell the truth in love; we must not expect too much of it; but we *must love:* "because the history of the world, which only stops at the half-house of love to bulldoze it into rubble, is ridiculous without it" (238). In fact, we must believe in love—as we must believe in objective truth—no

matter how strongly the evidence may be against it. Rushdie, who
has some qualms about the "critique" part of the novel, says this
about "Parenthesis":

> Barnes's view of history (voices echoing in the dark, etc.:
> near meaninglessness upon which we try to impose mean-
> ings) is, finally, what lets this book down; it's just too thin
> to support the whole fabric; but his view of love almost
> saves the day.[23]

The argument Barnes makes in "Parenthesis" is striking. Its
forcefulness, its shedding of the novelistic integument (unless we
decide that it is ironic, that the "Julian Barnes" speaking here is
a mask behind which the "real" Julian Barnes is smirking at the
sentimentality of these ideas), its broad claims—all these are
magisterial. On the other hand it is placed in a section called
"Parenthesis," which is only accorded half-chapter status, and it
is not at the end of the book, being followed by chapters 9 and 10.
How are readers to take it?

They should take it seriously, for Barnes means it. That does
not mean that it is entirely persuasive as an argument—it can be
beautiful and moving without the force to persuade. It is vulner-
able to charges of sentimentality or of old-fashioned liberal
humanism (surely Matthew Arnold's "Ah, love, let us be true to
one another"—as a spar to cling to in the wreckage of a meaning-
less world—is an unspoken source). It works to undermine the
postmodernist relativism to which the arguments about history

tend; if people tell the truth when they are in love, then there is truth to tell. Joyce Carol Oates carefully called Barnes a "quintessential humanist, of the pre-post-modernist species."[24] That is as good a description as any of the Julian Barnes who insists on the moral responsibility of art, who believes in good and evil, and who wrote *A History of the World in 10½ Chapters.*

CHAPTER EIGHT

Talking It Over

"Love and truth, that's the vital connection, love and truth," Julian Barnes insists in *A History of the World in 10½ Chapters.*[1] One of the three lovers in *Talking It Over* (1991) concludes that love—"or what people call love—is just a system for getting people to call you Darling after sex."[2] Barnes has returned to his great subject, love and its permutations, with special reference to infidelity and the triangular relationships created by an unfaithful wife, though he is interested again in alternative versions of events and the evanescence or inaccessibility of truth. The emotionally numbing aftereffects of cuckoldry were featured in *Flaubert's Parrot;* in *Before She Met Me* adultery and the suspicion of adultery and of past unfaithfulness drove the protagonist's deterioration; in *Metroland* the revelation that Chris's wife Marion has had an affair is quiet but jolting. In *Talking It Over* the plot presents a married couple and the successful machinations of the man's best friend to replace him in the marriage. Thus, despite Stuart's pessimistic reductionism about love, quoted above, the novel is a tribute to the power of love. Love makes Stuart change his life, twice; love makes Oliver renovate himself and become less an immature fop and more like an adult man; and love makes Gillian, the woman in dispute between them, act against her better judgment and against her will.

Oliver and Stuart are improbable best friends, being very different types. Stuart is a successful banker; Oliver is an unsuccessful teacher of English to foreigners in a squalid school. Stuart is a bit of a plodder, unadventurous, shy, and earnest; Oliver is dashing, quick, an ingratiating rogue. Stuart falls in love with and marries Gillian; the three spend much time together both before and after the wedding. But at the wedding Oliver is suddenly struck: *he is in love with Gillian.* He undertakes a well-planned, complicated, and expensive campaign to win her from Stuart and succeeds. They marry and move to France.[3] There is a final confrontation between Stuart and Gillian.

There is something classically simple, classically balanced about *Talking It Over.* (It is another triptych, like *Metroland* or *Staring at the Sun,* though divided among three dominant voices instead of into three interlocking sections.) There are only three important characters; they not only enact the plot but (with occasional stints by minor narrators such as Gillian's mother and father and a florist) narrate it, taking turns. The triangle is of a classic sort—a woman is "torn between two lovers": one of them, Stuart, is kind, reliable, well employed, but fairly dull; the other, Oliver, is handsome, witty, cultivated, charming, but irrespon- sible. There is something of Charles Bovary in Stuart, though Stuart is not so stupid and Gillian really loves him; and of Rodolphe in Oliver, though Oliver really loves Gillian and, after breaking up her marriage to Stuart, marries her. Unlike *Madame Bovary, Talking It Over* provides much less analysis of the woman's motives; Gillian does some talking, it is true, but she is at first unwilling to share her thoughts and then unable to explain what is happening to her.

The word *infidelity* suggests affairs, but in this novel the unfaithful lovers do not have a sexual affair. That is one of the surprises. Moreover, Oliver, apparently an accomplished seducer, *courts* Gillian—so successfully, indeed, that she first proposes their going to bed together, and he refuses. Their relations, though, are marked by betrayal and obsession, and the result is a strange reversal of Stuart and Oliver.

Clearly Gillian betrays Stuart when she falls in love with someone else, particularly with Stuart's best friend; clearly Oliver betrays Stuart by winning his wife away from him. It can be made more specific than that, though. Gillian, who gives this more thought than the men, recognizes that she has crossed a border when she begins keeping secrets from her husband(s). It begins when Oliver turns up at her door just after Stuart has gone to work, hands her a large bouquet of flowers, declares his love, and flees. She destroys the flowers and tells Stuart nothing about the visit. Later on, thinking over the advice about handling men that a friend of hers received from her mother—"It's always a good idea to keep them on the hop"—she reflects:

> What should I have done? If I were trying to keep things straight, I should have told Stuart about Oliver's appear-ance at the door and what I did with his flowers. But then should I also have said that Oliver rang up the next day and asked if I'd liked them? . . . No, presumably. So I made a joke . . . I'm not keeping him on the hop, but I am making a joke of things. This soon? (101)

After Stuart and Oliver have exchanged roles, Gillian reflects on "the first occasion you realize you can't, or at any rate you aren't going to, tell the man you've married everything. I had that with Oliver as I had it with Stuart" (260). What she is not telling

Oliver is about Stuart, just as what she did not tell Stuart was about Oliver.

Stuart has his own idea about when he was definitively betrayed. He and Gillian have always been embarrassed by the way they met, which was at a singles gathering that they had paid to attend. They have a cover story they use to keep everyone—and particularly Oliver, who has always belittled Stuart, especially about women—from knowing the truth. Oliver, inspired, alludes to the cover story about how Gillian and Stuart met: "Then she told me. Observe that I didn't have to ask. So it must be working the other way round as well: she's decided not to have any secrets from me either" (148). When Oliver, in turn, lets slip to Stuart that he knows the truth, Stuart takes it as "proof that she's having an affair with him—she betrayed me" (163).

Both Oliver and Stuart are obsessive about Gillian. The longer and more elaborate obsession is Oliver's. Once he falls in love with Gillian, on her wedding day, he is, as he inelegantly phrases it, "amazed, I'm overawed, I'm poo-scared, I'm mega-fuckstruck" (49). (Stuart reflects later that Oliver has never really been in love before, despite various claims and pretenses; he has certainly never felt this way.) Immediately he begins thinking about Gillian almost incessantly; he tries to find out where she and Stuart are going on their honeymoon, asking Stuart, then Gillian's mother; then he works out their return time and meets them at the airport, wearing a chauffeur's hat. As he does not relate, but both Stuart and Gillian do, he is a complete wreck, unwashed, drunk, nearly hysterical: during Gillian's absence he has fallen apart.

TALKING IT OVER

When Gillian and Stuart are returning from Boulogne after a weekend wandering aimlessly around France, Gillian sees Oliver on the ferry. He is uncharacteristically reticent, saying only that he got her home safely; but the only explanation is that he followed them throughout the weekend. Having seen him, Gillian keeps this knowledge from Stuart, another small act of betrayal or distancing from her husband.

Oliver rents a flat on the street where Stuart and Gillian live, to watch their movements—or mostly to watch Stuart, since Gillian, who restores paintings, works at home. Oliver is now free to phone or visit Gillian. He begins phoning her to tell her he loves her; though at first she always hangs up, she actually looks forward to the calls and presently stops hanging up. Soon Oliver is spending his days with Gillian; he watches her work, talks with her (quietly and honestly, eschewing his usual flash and insincerity), combs her hair. It is all very romantic; when one day Gillian, "burning," takes him in her arms and invites him to bed, he refuses because he does not want to have an affair with her; "'I want all of you,' he said. 'I don't want part of you. I want the lot'" (150).

Gillian's obsession with Oliver develops more slowly and of course is largely a matter of enlarged permissions rather than crafty stratagems; from receiving his avowals of love in silence, the stages are clear. When she keeps the secret of having seen Oliver on the Boulogne ferry, she thinks: "What's happening? It's not my fault, but I feel guilty. . . . I don't know if I did the right thing, either. Maybe I shouldn't have done anything. Maybe what I did was an act of complicity, or looked as if it could have been"

(107). Soon, though she still puts the phone down on Oliver, she thinks: "I know why I feel guilty. Perhaps you guessed. I feel guilty because I find Oliver attractive" (116). Once she begins making comparisons between the two men, Stuart is finished: he lacks charm, he is unaware that he is competing, he is no longer courting Gillian, and (as he bitterly reflects later) since unlike Oliver he has a job to go to, he is not around all day long. Presently she thinks, "despite the fact that I love Stuart, I seem to be falling in love with Oliver" (144).

The story moves rapidly to its reversal. Stuart spots Oliver on the street, learns about his secret life, and confronts him. Oliver confesses to loving Gillian; Stuart head-butts him into the emergency room; Stuart begs Gillian not to leave. The next event is the wedding of Oliver and Gillian.

The result is that *Stuart* is now obsessed. His motives are more mixed than Oliver's: he feels enormous shame (partly as a result of his marriage having ended after only a few months, which he believes will make people think he was sexually inadequate); enormous anger; enormous disillusionment. He toys with various plans for revenge, but what he eventually does is much more like Oliver. He travels to France and rents a room near their home so he can watch them from his window, as Oliver used to watch him and Gillian. He is finally assuaged by a bit of theatrics arranged by Gillian to make it look as if she is miserable in her new marriage, which seems to make him happy.

The way Stuart duplicates Oliver's spying scheme exemplifies the pattern of reversal in this novel. If Gillian is the unmoving pivot, Stuart and Oliver are the moving parts that exchange position. The most obvious way, of course, is that Oliver replaces

Stuart as Gillian's husband, though, rather oddly, they seem to hope that after they are married Stuart will go on being their friend—that he will take on Oliver's abandoned role. Stuart recognizes the pattern of symmetries and reversals; having determined to go to Oliver and Gillian's wedding, he says, "He came to mine. Why shouldn't I go to his?" (197). At the very end of the novel, Stuart's French landlady observes that "he hadn't even told us his real name. He'd changed it" (274). This is the Stuart who says in chapter 1 that *"everyone else around here has changed their name"*(4; actually Gillian reveals much later that she never took Stuart's name upon marriage, though he thought she did).

Stuart and Oliver also partially exchange characters, or personalities. Oliver is a heavy drinker and smoker as the novel begins; he becomes more abstemious, even giving up smoking. Stuart takes up Oliver's smoking habit—literally, in fact: he has brought French cigarettes back from the weekend break to give to Oliver; when Gillian tells him that Oliver has given up the habit—as part of his new life designed to appeal to Gillian, though of course she does not explain it to Stuart this way—he smokes them instead and develops a major habit (when he intrudes on Gillian and Oliver's wedding reception, he seems to have two cigarettes lit.) Though never a teetotaler, Stuart becomes a drunk as his marriage dissolves, while Oliver develops responsibility in his alcohol consumption as in other sectors of his life. Oliver has been the one with frequent casual affairs; in the second half of the novel the divorced Stuart develops this habit, though he prefers paid companionship, having decided cynically that love is an illusion and money can buy it.

The relationship between love and money is both another aspect of the reversal of roles and one of the important themes of this novel. In the beginning Stuart has plenty of money and Oliver does not. They disagree on the wording but concur that the first words ever spoken between them were Oliver's request that Stuart lend him money.

Oliver, who has a gift for metaphorical flights and who, from time to time, condescendingly tries to speak in Stuart's frame of reference—which he takes to be ignorant, materialistic, and mercantile—uses a financial conceit to explain his takeover of Gillian—in the major confrontation at the center of the book—blaming the whole thing on market forces. To Stuart's complaint that love and money are two different things, Oliver responds:

> "Ah, but there are such parallels, Stuart. They both go where they wist, reckless of what they leave behind. Love too has its buy-outs, its asset stripping, its junk bonds. Love rises and falls in value like any currency. And confidence is *such* a key to maintaining its value.... Money, as I further understand it, is morally neutral." (160)

The parallel can go further: Oliver announces his plans to make an offer for Gillian, which he knows will be accepted by the "board," that is, Gillian. And he acknowledges the irony that he, the "classical humanist of artistic bent and romantic nature" (161), is talking of love in economic terms, while Stuart, the banker, finds the analogy horrifying.

As we would expect, Oliver changes his mind about this, rejecting the analogy of love and money; but by this time Stuart has grown to accept it, or a sour version of it:

> So you see, in a way I've come round to Oliver's point of view, to what he was insultingly trying to explain to me when we were both drunk and I ended up nutting him. Love operates according to market forces, he said, as a justification for stealing my wife. Now, a bit older and a bit wiser, I'm beginning to agree: love does have many of the same properties as money. (235)

As a materialist, Stuart has come to think of love as an illusion the value of which, like the value of money, is sustained so long as everyone agrees to grant it a value; and insofar as love just equals sex (the downright materialist conclusion), money and love *are* equivalents in the market.

The symmetry of Barnes's triangular arrangement of his characters goes beyond these neat reversals. Oliver and Stuart have a strong relationship that is more than loving the same woman and partially survives their struggle over her. Not only are they friends from their school days who remain close (despite their many differences) in adult London life, but they have a symbiotic relationship. Oliver, before Gillian, used to help Stuart get dates; Stuart, who has always had more money, used to pay for these dates and give Oliver other financial support. Oliver depends on Stuart's dullness and predictability and lack of sparkle to make him seem more interesting; Stuart seems to need

Oliver less, but perhaps Oliver's worldly failure and bad habits make Stuart seem—at least to himself—more grown-up and realistic. In France, Oliver thinks, "There are times when I miss Stuart" (252); and Gillian quite realistically suggests that "here the only English person he's got to set him off is me, and that's not really enough. He needed someone like Stuart around" (258).

In one of the few sections of the novel of any length or importance voiced by someone other than the three principals, a woman named Val gives her interpretation of the triangle. She is well placed to comment since, according to her, she is one of Stuart's old lovers whom Oliver tried to steal away, in an apparent parallel or anticipation of the main action of the novel. And her interpretation is that Oliver is "queer for Stuart":

> That's why he's always put Stuart down, laughing at how shabby and boring he is. He puts Stuart down so that neither of them will have to admit what's always been there, what might be there if they didn't play the game of Stuart being shabby and boring and such an unlikely companion for flash Oliver. (185)

This one, like almost every other opinion in the book, is qualified by being only one person's view, and it is contradicted by both Stuart and Oliver. But then, as Val would say, they *would* deny it, wouldn't they?

Thinking about Val is a good way to approach the unusual narrative procedure of *Talking It Over*. What are readers to make of her analysis of Oliver's homosexual attraction to Stuart? How intelligent is she? How reliable? (Stuart reveals that she is the manager of a photocopy shop; Oliver says that she has not even given her real name—but then again neither does he.) The anonymous reviewer for *Private Eye* comments, "For a start it's all written in dialogue, so you can never decide who's telling the truth and who isn't."[4] This is not quite right; it is not written in dialogue but *monologues.* All the narrators speak directly to the reader. D. J. Taylor writes dismissively, "Ask what *Talking It Over* is 'about' and the answer is, that frightful chestnut, the subjective nature of truth: the impossibility of working out who did what to whom at a particular time."[5] The echo here of Barnes's own comments about *Before She Met Me* is striking; commenting on that book, he said that "what is constant is the human heart and human passions. And the change in who does what with whom—that's a superficial change."[6] It is hardly superficial in *Talking It Over:* the change in who does what with whom, and the reasons for and consequences of that change, *is the book.* And it can only be so when readers can tell who does what with, or to, whom. Stuart marries Gillian, and then Oliver marries her: that is crystalline. Each of Barnes's books since *Flaubert's Parrot* has been identified by somebody as being about the subjective nature of truth; whether this is taken to be a good thing varies from one review to another, depending on the critic's own views of truth—in other words, the value placed on this alleged theme is itself subjective.

But this is not really what the books are *about.* There is a great deal of subjectivity and uncertainty in *Talking It Over,* as there is in *Flaubert's Parrot* and *A History of the World in 10½ Chapters;* but readers can, in fact, work out with some certainty who did what to whom. One incident cited in *Private Eye* is the collision of Stuart's head with Oliver's; Stuart says he head-butted, or nutted, Oliver; Oliver tells the reader that it was "an unfortunate clash of heads" when Stuart was lighting Oliver's cigarette, and he ignored the blood and went to bed. But Gillian has a voice here too, and her story is that Oliver, who needed five stitches in his cheek, described the violence on Stuart's face as terrifying. Oliver wants sympathy from Gillian and wants to alienate her from Stuart, but he wants sympathy from the reader as well. When Stuart reveals that Oliver is generally a coward, and much the larger of the two men, one is able to settle what really happened in this case with some confidence. Gillian's words usually tend to provide a "better" picture of Stuart than one gets from Oliver—making sure readers realize, for instance, that Stuart is perfectly good in bed, that he is less hapless than Oliver enjoys thinking, that he behaves very generously over the divorce; and they undermine Oliver's own self-portrayal as always suave and charming, revealing that he is greasy and panicky, that the car he thinks shows such panache is "that stupid old tank he drives because he thinks it's stylish" (257).

This is not to suggest that everything is clear and certain. After all, the characters do not always know themselves with certainty; they play roles with each other and the reader; they wonder who is right and wrong; and they view events through their own self-interest: for example, in one brief chapter, when they realize the complications they are in, each says, "I'm the one that's going to get hurt"(129–30). Clearly they cannot each be "the one." Here is one of those contradictions of which *Talking It Over* is made up. But is this one of those questions that the reader simply cannot answer? Is this a subjective truth? Surely it becomes obvious that Stuart is the one who is *really* going to get hurt. When they say this, Oliver and Gillian are wrong. They are not lying but rather experiencing the usual self-regard and anxiety typical of our species. As things work out, even they would be willing to admit that neither of them was "the one" who got hurt. Triangulation is a way of achieving a rough knowledge, and the reader of this novel knows with considerable accuracy who did what to whom.

Arriving at a comfortable judgment of the events is much harder. Who was right, and who was wrong? The three main characters disagree about this. Mme. Wyatt, Gillian's mother, has a view, which is subtler and more fatalistic than theirs. Val, whose analysis is accompanied by a good deal of spite that must be factored into the reader's reception of it, provides a theory that (since both Stuart and Oliver love Gillian) has to come from outside the triangle:

> if I were you I'd take a closer look at Gillian. Isn't she just a heroine, isn't she such a little *coper*? . . . Gillian gets trapped in a Love Triangle and guess which of the three comes out the best? Well, it's Little Miss Who. Caught in the middle and still keeping her head above water while doing the right thing—which means shredding Stuart and keeping Oliver on a string. (189)

She even suggests that Gillian planned the whole thing, made a play for Oliver without his realizing it; "that's her trick. She hasn't been doing it to you, has she?" (190). In a way she has. All of them have, including Val.

The novel consists of a series of different voices that contradict, qualify, support, and augment each other's accounts. What
is unusual about this is their naked appeal to the reader for
sympathy and agreement. Readers may be accustomed to having
narrators who speak directly to them (think of Jane Eyre's
"Reader, I married him"), even multiple narrators doing it. The
woodworm in *A History of the World in 10½ Chapters* does it.
Geoffrey Braithwaite does it in *Flaubert's Parrot,* for instance
when he acknowledges the reader's suspicion that he may have
killed Ellen: "No, I didn't kill my wife. I might have known you'd
think that."[7] But the imagined relationship between reader and
narrator in this book is much closer. Each "talks it over" with the
reader, or imagined listener, in turn; each is aware that the others
are also talking; each makes some appeal to the reader for help.
The reader is figured as interacting with the characters; Stuart
starts to tell what Gillian looks like, then says "She . . . well,
you've seen her for yourself, haven't you?" (37). As things fall
apart he says, "Of course I'm drunk. Wouldn't you be?" (143).
Gillian admits that she is aroused by Oliver's phone calls: "And
do you know what's started happening? As I put the phone down
I feel wet. Can you imagine it?" (145).

   That these are not just rhetorical questions, that the narrative
scheme of this novel is meant to be more interactive, is shown by
Oliver's hunger for sympathy (ostensibly the most confident, he
is also the most needy for approval):

   I probably shouldn't be telling you all this if I want to keep
   your sympathy. (Have I got it in the first place? Hard to tell,
   I'd say. And do I want it? I do, I do!) It's just that I'm too

involved in what's happening to play games—at least, to play games with you. I'm fated to carry on with what I have to do and hope not to incur your terminal disapproval in the process. Promise not to turn your face away: if *you* decline to perceive me, then I really *shall* cease to exist. Don't kill me off! Spare poor Ollie and he may yet amuse you! (88)

This puts the matter of "sympathy" with fictional characters in a stronger light and raises interesting philosophical questions, of the tree-falling-in-the-forest variety, about the ontology of fictional creations. It is self-conscious fiction: Oliver earlier acknowledges he is in a book, or at least that he could not go through a whole book being called Nigel (his childhood name). In a sense, then, if readers "sympathize" with Gillian, Val is right: she *has* worked her trick on them. Her technique is reticence and self-protection, while Oliver's is open pleading and a showy rhetorical display; Stuart's is just telling his story, with the aid of his excellent memory, and hoping for justice: this did not work out in his marriage, but it just might keep the affections of a reader.

Later things become even odder. In the last section, with Oliver and Gillian living in France, Gillian asks the reader: "Just out of interest, do you think Oliver's been faithful to me since we were married? Sorry, that's neither here nor there" (270). Oliver has asked a similar question, though surprisingly about Stuart: "Do you know if he's got a girl? I wonder if he's got some crepuscular secret, some sexual hidey-hole" (253).

The strangest behavior among the characters occurs when Val is ejected by Stuart and Oliver. On her first "appearance" she provides some background on Stuart and Oliver and offers her opinion that Oliver is "queer for Stuart" and then says "I'm off now. You won't be seeing me again, not unless there's a real turn-up for the book" (183).[8] Since both men contradict her, with some vilification, she does speak twice more in this chapter; then, surprisingly, she reappears after the wedding, predicting doom, repeating her idea of Oliver's sexual interests, calling Gillian a "prim ballcrusher." Oliver and Stuart join forces to remove her from the book, despite her forceful appeals to the reader: "Hey *you*—aren't you meant to be the manager. . . . Can't you see what's going on? This is a direct challenge to your authority. Help me. Please"; she even offers to reveal the two men's sexual secrets in return for the reader's help (219–20). Stuart and Oliver gag her with a scarf. This sort of behavior, perhaps, led Christopher Hudson to conclude that "Reading this book is like being trapped in a pub theatre with a fringe drama group grimly intent on audience participation."[9]

Despite pretended struggles with scarves or smoking, though, and despite what they reveal about what they have done and suffered, all *Talking It Over* contains is really just voices: "Barnes has ditched authorial narrative in favour of three competing and contrasting addresses to the reader."[10] The author's ventriloquistic creation of these three very different voice-personalities is a matter of vocabulary, references, reticences, syntax, and cadence. Stuart's was presumably the most difficult as well as the most important; as an unclever, unimaginative man, not much of a reader, who never went to university, he is unable to use much of what makes Julian Barnes's own literary voice rich. Stuart's language is more commonplace than readers are

TALKING IT OVER

accustomed to in a Julian Barnes novel; he knows that he is not good at jokes or figurative flights and prides himself mostly on his good memory.

By contrast, Oliver pretends to have forgotten even the name of their school, and his voice is entirely different too—foppish, learned, showy, precious. His analogies—life is like invading Russia, love is like money, affairs are like time-shares—are amusing. He pretentiously refers to his father working the "*mots croisés*" in the paper. He enjoys finding different ways to make fun of Stuart: "Let me zero my telepathy in on the benign, rumpled and somewhat steatopygous figure of my friend Stu" (25). At Gatwick he reports, "Stuart had typically picked a trolley with one locked wheel, and he emerged from the tender scrutiny of the *douaniers* in a comic curve, his uncertain course hymned by Gillian's indulgent laughter and his trolley's maundering squeak" (67). [11] He decorates his style with far-fetched cultural allusions, until finally, near the end, he says, "It was just like . . . oh, fill in your own fucking opera reference for a change. I'm fed up doing all the work" (272). Zoe Heller comments penetratingly on this pair of voices:

> Stuart—a plodder, teetering on the edge of full-blown wallyhood—unknowingly speaks his vulnerability from the start, and it is his hidden reserves of toughness that take a while to emerge. Oliver is a clever dick—so well-read that he can afford to be wittily irreverent about art and philosophy. He makes much of his effortless glamour, but by the end of the novel his grooviness seems about as spontaneous as one of Stuart's soirées. [12]

UNDERSTANDING JULIAN BARNES

Readers can hardly help being dazzled by Oliver; Anthony Quinn describes him as "at once the most entertaining and the most problematic side of the triangle," who "charms the pants off us as well as Gill" with his "preening *hauteur*,"[13] though his excesses become wearying, as even he realizes. He is always trying too hard. There is a bit of his author in him. One of his favorite words is "crepuscular"; he overuses it, at one point promises the reader to stop saying it, then goes back to it later on: "And yes, I do know I've just said *crepuscular* again" (196). In the introduction to *Letters from London,* Barnes includes a conversation with his editor at *The New Yorker* centered on his use of "one of those words like, say, *crepuscular* or *inspissated,* which don't form part of your vocabulary but which you reach for from time to time."[14]

Some reviewers found Oliver less like Julian Barnes than like Gregory Service, one of the speakers in the divided narrative of Martin Amis's 1977 novel *Success,* also about a triangular relationship with two men, one plodding and one showy.[15] There is an undoubted resemblance between the plots of the two novels and between the style of Oliver Russell and Gregory Service, which may be slyly acknowledged in Oliver's insistence, from time to time, that a car is *not* a Lagonda—a car emblematic of style and flash in Amis's work. The significance of any borrowing seems to have been magnified by the feeling in some members of the reviewing establishment that Amis and Barnes were part of some overpraised club of trickster-novelists. D. J. Taylor follows his complaint about the intertextual use of *Success* with an odd but amusing fancy:

> I, for one, am mildly disillusioned with these attempts to
> grapple with the big issues that the novel demands of a

writer of Barnes's skill, which merely feint (or faint) away into the eachway bet of jolly contrivance. In fact, it would be a good idea if Barnes and Amis minor, and one or two other bright boys, were set down in a locked study and not allowed to come out until they had written a 400-page family saga featuring a small boy with a pony named Jonjo. The joke is that they would probably do it rather well.[16]

This seems a fogyish blast in the ongoing British argument about the validity of modernism and postmodernism. Philip Howard also thinks of Barnes as a teaser of the reader, but he offers a more generous summary of *Talking It Over:*

It is, of course, quick-silver clever and allusive, funny about things that nobody else bothers to write about, such as the snobberies of food and gents' lavatory etiquette at the urinal. Its cultural credentials are brilliant. It is funny, but also very sad. The message, in an analogy that recurs, that money is a better bet than that tricky old currency love, cannot be right. But then, that is only one of the possible readings.[17]

The key point is that cleverness, allusiveness, and cultural credentials are not enough. At the heart of the novel is the subject Barnes identified as motivating *Before She Met Me:* "what is constant is the human heart and human passions," though it would be impossible to agree, about this novel, with "the change in who does what with whom—that's a superficial change."[18]

The mixture of comedy and sadness is a key to the contents of *Talking It Over.* Like *Before She Met Me,* it is funny all the way, or almost all the way, through; like that novel, it tells a sad story. There is no happy ending in sight—or rather, the happiness of the ending varies according to which of the trio is talking. Oliver is probably most satisfied, though even he has found that despite winning the woman he loves his life shows signs of dullness. Gillian is even more unromantic about her current life and about Oliver. Only Stuart can be said to be happy, and his happiness arises from a purely local and falsified event: when Gillian starts a furious quarrel with Oliver in the street, knowing that Stuart is watching, the conviction that they are miserable gives him some pleasure. The final *event* of the book is actually the death of a doe.

In Barnes's next novel, while he did not write about the donkey Jonjo, he turned to something much less "tricky" and produced a novel that lacks quicksilver cleverness, allusiveness, "brilliance," and even much wit. Like each book before it, it is a new departure.

CHAPTER NINE

The Porcupine

The Porcupine is Julian Barnes's first novel to appear first in a language other than English; what is almost as surprising is that the language it appeared in first was not French, but Bulgarian. It was published by Obsidian of Sofia in 1992 under the title of *Bodlivo Svinche* and was an immediate sensation, selling ten thousand copies in hardback and being recommended on the television news.[1] Once the book had been published in English, readers were able to discover that Julian Barnes had once again defied expectations. One reviewer wrote: "To those who have never imagined Barnes as a political writer, this book will come as a revelation."[2]

It is true that politics, either domestic or international, have played little role in most of Barnes's novels: there is a discussion of democracy in *Flaubert's Parrot,* but it is largely theoretical and turns on a justification of Flaubert's disdain for democracy; there are the *événements* of Paris 1968 in *Metroland,* but the point is that Christopher was too busy with Annick to be aware that he was living through them. Jack's suggestion in *Before She Met Me* that the reptilian brain makes people "vote Tory, kick the dog" contains a political view, although in a throwaway line.[3] Political themes emerge from time to time in *A History of the World in 10½ Chapters,* but never in a way to suggest that Barnes thinks they are important. One short story, "One of a Kind," assumes some knowledge of the political situation in Romania, but it is hardly a political fiction.

UNDERSTANDING JULIAN BARNES

The expectation that a British writer will have a political stance is usually a demand for an open commitment to the broad Left. Despite shifting allegiances since 1979, one still finds the belief that writers and artists and intellectuals should feel, and express in their art, a solidarity with the working class. To hear an artist of Barnes's age admit to voting Conservative is unusual, whatever they may actually do at the polls. Thus politics ordinarily appears in recent English literature as anti-Thatcherism, anti-imperialism (with these two goes a considerable amount of anti-Americanism), opposition to the Poll Tax, support for striking miners, and so on. Antiracism and feminism are frequent themes, as was, until 1989 or so, a view that the United States and the U.S.S.R. were rough moral equivalents, that triumphal U.S.-style consumerist capitalism and Soviet Communism were two objectionable—perhaps equally objectionable—ideologies.

Many writers have never subscribed to this package of political positions. Tom Stoppard, for instance, whose history as a refugee from totalitarianism in Czechoslovakia may explain his suspicion, long resisted the demand that his plays demonstrate a political engagement, a demand based on the widely shared credo that all art is political and that apparently nonpolitical art is simply reactionary. Barnes, who began publishing novels in 1980, missed the most febrile years of politicization of art. He is, moreover, a man of the Left, who campaigned for Labour in 1992. Yet most of his novels are nonpolitical. One explanation may be provided by Geoffrey Braithwaite, answering the case

THE PORCUPINE

against Flaubert and specifically the complaint that he was not interested enough in politics:

> *Literature includes politics, and not vice versa.* This isn't a fashionable view, neither with writers nor politicians, but you will forgive me. Novelists who think their writing an instrument of politics seem to me to degrade writing and foolishly exalt politics. No, I'm not saying they should be forbidden from having political opinions or from making political statements. It's just that they should call that part of their work journalism. The writer who imagines that the novel is the most effective way of taking part in politics is usually a bad novelist, a bad journalist, and a bad politician.[4]

Still, *The Porcupine* is about politics. One reason for the change of subject matter may have been impatience with England. In an article called "Where Nothing Really Happens," critic William Leith examines the shortcomings of the country, which—partly as a result of novelists who write about elsewhere—"appears less *... interesting.* Less ... *mythic.* Less like a place where important things are happening. And you wonder—if England seems a more diluted, washed-out kind of country these days, maybe that's because it *is.*"[5] Asked about his choice of an Eastern European political situation for *The Porcupine,* Barnes replied: "There's no point in doing a little-England version of the American novel—the Empire is long dead. What is London the centre of in the world? Symphony orchestras, maybe. Symphony orchestras and royalty. But that doesn't make me want to write a novel about the Royal Family. . . ."[6] Leith diagnoses a feeling that English experience is somehow belated and that English politics are somehow irrelevant (the Royal Family); for many British intellectuals the 1992 general election, in which the uninspiring John Major and his Tories won a comfortable victory over the Labour Party despite thirteen years of economic decline, frustration, and growing unpopularity, made them despair. Barnes may not have despaired, but, as he shows in *Letters from London,* he campaigned for Labour and views the Conservatives as almost inexplicable—harsh and dogmatic under Thatcher, befuddled and inept under Major, darkly comic all the time. That they remain in power must frustrate him. It has recently seemed to many that British politics have grown futile: the electorate could not even manage to change the party in power, while in Eastern Europe whole societies were moving from entrenched Marxism to something like western-style liberal democracy, the market economy, and civil freedoms. While Britain was led by a barely educated nonentity distinguished for colorless rhetoric, whose most ardent political commitment was to providing more toilets along the motorway, Czechoslovakia had not only chosen freedom but elected an intellectual, a playwright who had been imprisoned for his beliefs, as president. *Eastern Europe* was where something was really happening.

In addition to focusing on a Communist country in transition to a capitalist-democratic state, *The Porcupine* is a strikingly different kind of novel for Julian Barnes. There is nothing postmodern about it; it is not tricky, or experimental, or dazzling, or even—barring a few wry inventions—particularly witty.

Whether the topic helped to dictate a more somber approach is hard to say. John Bayley points out that:

> At a time when the novel—and above all a novel by someone like Julian Barnes—is supposed to be quite different from anything humdrum that is actually happening, *The Porcupine* seems to attempt to break the mold.
>
> In doing so it forfeits the puckish individuality of Barnes's previous novels, adopting instead with an almost military rigor the techniques of "committed" fiction, as it used to be practiced by André Malraux, George Orwell, and Arthur Koestler.[7]

Bayley's reaction is not particularly enthusiastic, and other critics had real reservations about Barnes's success in his new endeavor: for some, the political ideas were obvious; for others, they were wrong and even dangerous; others just missed the old Julian Barnes, with his playfulness and humor and quicksilver invention.

Bayley's comparing Barnes to "committed" authors of the democratic Left is interesting, that is, interestingly mistaken, partly because it helps to measure how very far from that sort of commitment Barnes actually is. He does not, of course, suggest that a country like Bulgaria (and *The Porcupine* is set in a country very much like Bulgaria and based on some of its recent history[8]) would be better off if its Communist leadership had never fallen; he does, however, demonstrate uncomfortably that there are no gains without losses, that virtue and vice are not easily distinguishable or exclusively distributed, and that the end of Communism brings its own woes and moral compromises. The novel confronts the new system with the old and shows that they are more balanced than one might expect, or hope; it would be possible to read the novel as suggesting nearly moral equivalence between Bolshevism and liberalism.[9]

The Porcupine is the simplest of all Julian Barnes's novels. It begins after the former Communist dictator of the country has been overthrown and imprisoned, his government replaced by a struggling democracy. Now the deposed Leader, Stoyo Petkanov, is to be tried. His prosecutor is an ambitious former Party member, Peter Solinsky, who has a multitude of reasons for wanting to convict Petkanov: these include genuine national feeling; his own ambition; and the fact that his father, a former high government official, was purged by Petkanov. In the course of this short novel Solinsky prepares for the trial, it takes place, and Petkanov is convicted.

There is little suspense; it is clear both that Petkanov has done enough to be convicted of something and that even if he has not, he must be convicted anyway. As the head of Patriotic Security Forces (renamed from the discredited Department of Internal Security) explains to prosecutor Solinsky: "It is important to hold this trial, for the good of the nation. It is equally important that the accused be found guilty."[10] In fact it is embarrassingly close to being a show trial in the old-fashioned Stalinist sense. Charging Petkanov proves to be difficult, since almost everything he did was legal by definition; he is eventually tried for minor and largely irrelevant offenses, including misuse of royalties on his speeches and giving and receiving undeserved benefits, or financial corruption. It is acknowledged that the real charge cannot be brought because there were no laws against it; to his bitterest enemies, Petkanov is being tried for "*Mass murder. Genocide. Ruining the country*" (32); in his defense, he defines the charges quite differently:

> I am charged with bringing peace and prosperity and international respect to this country. I am charged with uprooting Fascism, with abolishing unemployment, with building schools and hospitals and hydro-electric dams. I am charged with being a Socialist and a Communist. Guilty, comrades, in every case. (121)

The peculiarly *un*committed quality of *The Porcupine* has several explanations. One is the persons who are the representatives of old and new, of communism and postcommunism.

Stoyo Petkanov is probably the monster his enemies believe him to be. He has been ruthless; he is unchanged in his contempt for weakness (he particularly despises Gorbachev); he rejects the concept of freedom; he hates the capitalist system, for which his shorthand is Mickey Mouse and Frank Sinatra. He has retrograde views on women—much of the trouble in the world he traces to men too weak to control their women, and he puts Gorbachev and Reagan at the head of this category.

Yet there is something charismatic and powerful about Petkanov as well. He is a compelling speaker, and his spirited defense in court, though unavailing as he knows it will be, is stirring. He has had some successes; he is able to point out that when he was in charge the people had food to eat and nobody was "selling pornography outside the Mausoleum of the First Leader" (81). Moreover, he is uncorrupted by doubt. He is sure that he is in the right and treats his trial, his captors, and the new leaders of his country with disdain. In fact he is serenely confident that socialism has not failed, only fallen short at the first jump. When he says that "Socialism is not built without sacrifice," he is narrowly justifying his purging of Solinsky's father, but there is a broader application, which is important to the philosophical dialectic of this novel. That is, Petkanov, and Marxism generally, believe that the end justifies the means. He asks Peter Solinsky, "What do people want? They want stability and hope. We gave them that. Things might not have been perfect, but with Socialism people could dream that one day they might be" (69). For the compromises, mistakes, errors necessary in pursuing these goals, the Leader accepts responsibility. Stoyo Petkanov makes a powerful impact in this book not just because Barnes has made him easily the most impressive character, and because—to be fair— he does have a case, but also because of the weakness and ambiguity of his opposition.

Peter Solinsky begins with a righteous conviction that he is right and Petkanov is wrong, and a naive feeling that he can understand and persuade the old dictator to see and admit his own wrongdoing. Petkanov does not change; Solinsky does. He is already compromised, like almost everybody in power, because he is a former party member whose position of importance was gained under the old regime; in other words, he and the others have changed their spots—Petkanov has not. After his conviction, the former "helmsman" reads out a long list of decorations he has received from all over the world, including capitalist, communist, and neutral countries, and testimonials to him from people such as Jimmy Carter, the secretary general of the UN, and the king of Spain. Though the dictator cites them more or less as character references, Barnes's larger suggestion seems to be that the consciences of his critics are hardly clean.[11]

Compromised in his new role by having recently been a Communist, Solinsky was also compromised *as* a Communist; once, sent to Turin with a trade delegation (a sign that the government trusted him), he spent the hard currency with which he was entrusted on an expensive suit, whiskey, and an Italian woman, whom he took to dinner and later to his hotel for the night. Petkanov tells this story in open court (and thus on television) to make his rhetorical point: "Tell me, what is corruption? I congratulate you. I have seen the photographs" (86).

Already flawed before the trial begins, Solinsky corrupts himself further. First he loses his planned objectivity and develops a genuine hatred for his prey: "His loathing had become personal, furious, snobbish and corroding. Past shame, present detestation, future fear: the mix had begun to consume the prosecutor" (103). And then he acts dishonestly himself; the need to convict Petkanov is so great that he is willing to use tainted evidence: a document, probably forged, that seems to show Petkanov's approval of "all necessary means" against state enemies. The prosecution is able to link this with the deaths of exiled political opponents and even Petkanov's daughter:

> You killed your daughter, Mr Petkanov, and you are here before us as the representative and chief director of a political system under which it is *entirely legal,* in your

much-repeated phrase, *entirely legal* for the head of state to authorise the death even of one of his own ministers, in this case Anna Petkanova, the Minister of Culture. (111)

The fact that the charge is probably not true, that the document is probably a forgery, has become less important than the need for a conviction. The end justifies the means. Challenged by his disgusted wife, Peter Solinsky thinks "The document is true, even if it is a forgery. Even if it isn't true, it is necessary" (113). Where have readers heard this reasoning before? While it may sound something like the justification offered on behalf of totalitarianism in George Orwell's *1984* or Yevgeny Zamyatin's *We,* it sounds even more like Duffy's ethical code:

Duffy, like most coppers, had a slightly flexible approach to the truth. You had to if you wanted to survive: not survive as a copper, but survive within yourself. . . . Sometimes, for instance, it might be necessary to tell a little lie . . . in order to make sure that a much bigger lie didn't get to pass itself off as the truth. On those occasions you felt bad for a bit, though you knew you didn't have any choice in the matter.[12]

Peter Solinsky has forfeited the moral advantage over Stoyo Petkanov; Michiko Kakutani argues that "By the novel's conclusion, the reader has realized that the initials of the two men are the same (though reversed), that Petkanov and Solinsky are, in fact, alter egos of one another."[13] To Solinsky's annoyance, Petkanov recognizes this fact too.

And what is worse, Peter Solinsky, once he has lost the moral advantage over Stoyo Petkanov, can only be an *inferior* Stoyo

THE PORCUPINE

Petkanov. Petkanov has always believed that ends justify means—moreover his ends, as he defines them, are noble ones like building dams, ending starvation, and defeating fascism. Of course, to a political pragmatist, these justify purging Peter Solinsky's father or repressing dissident elements. So, even though the particular document was probably a forgery, Stoyo's ideology would justify the use of "all necessary means" against state enemies.

Peter Solinsky is meant to be the embodiment of a more humane, limited political ethos. He is shocked, or pretends to be, by the "all necessary means" clause. But he is willing to use all necessary means to convict Petkanov. And not only is this at odds with what he believes, or thinks he believes, or used to believe, but the end that supposedly justifies him is not defeating fascism and feeding the hungry but achieving a conviction, on dubious and minor charges, of a sick old man.

At the center of *The Porcupine* is the confrontation between Solinsky and Petkanov, but there are important functions for the other characters, most of them, in effect, chorus figures. At one extreme is a group of young students, who were in the anticommunist uprising from the beginning and who come together to watch the trial on television, make sardonic comments, and demand execution for Petkanov. At the other is the grandmother of Stefan, one of the students, who is a patient and dedicated communist and who has a picture of Lenin on her wall, keeping silent witness to the truths of the class struggle. In her mind, liberalization means a return to fascism and the oppression of the workers. She keeps the faith; the novel closes with a vignette of her, after Petkanov's conviction and sentencing, standing in the rain in front of the Mausoleum of the First Leader (now empty), clutching her picture of Lenin, indifferent to the shouts of drunks or students: "she stood her ground, and she remained silent" (138). The dignity of the old woman and her placement at the end of the novel give some weight to the suggestion that Barnes sees no progress in the movement from communism to a freer society.

She and the students are the uncomplicated true believers. A more complex position is that of Peter Solinsky's wife Maria; the daughter of a hero of the antifascist struggle, she is more cautious than her husband. Doubtful of his motives from the beginning, she has nothing but contempt for him by the end of the novel because of his plunge into the iniquity of which he was supposed to be the scourge. The marriage of the Solinskys is, considering Barnes's usual interests, sketchy; the important point is that after his changes, she not only does not love him but can no longer respect him.

An even more influential judgment is that of the Devinsky Commando, a group of ironic protesters who had been at the forefront of the student demonstrations that doomed the old regime. Named after a poet who wrote an ironic "loyal sonnet" called "Thank You, Your Majesty," they parody extreme devotion, wearing the headgear of Young Pioneers and chanting slogans like "THANK YOU FOR THE PRICE RISES. THANK YOU FOR THE FOOD SHORTAGES. GIVE US IDEOLOGY NOT BREAD" (46). The Devinsky Commando is a powerful force, as irony is a subtle weapon against totalitarianism. The ironies multiply: the officer who was ordered to disperse the demonstration ends up being kissed by a student, and thus becomes a symbol of the revolution without quite understanding his own motives; by the time of the trial, he is the head of the Patriotic Security Forces, the spokesman for the necessity of convicting Petkanov whether guilty or not, and the source of the forged document that dooms the old dictator. And after the trial Peter Solinsky receives an anonymous postcard, presumably from the Commando, which used to demand "GIVE US IDEOL-OGY NOT BREAD," reading "GIVE US CONVICTIONS NOT JUSTICE!" (127).

The Devinsky Commando is one of the few sprightly evidences of the Barnes playfulness in this book, and it must be said that, if the new interest in politics and moral obliquities in Eastern Europe requires the sacrifice of the usual Barnes touch, it is a high price to pay, perhaps too high. Robert Stone writes that "In much of his other work, Julian Barnes has approached the novel with shrewdly self-conscious obliqueness. In *The Porcupine* he consents to play the game. But a novel of such ambitious purview requires a greater density of language and ambiance than the author allows time for."[14] There is, indeed, something thin about this novel, which is also one of his shortest. Some of the concerns on which Barnes is always acute elude readers here, including the complexities of love and the relations between art and life.[15] Aside from Stoyo Petkanov, no character, not even Solinsky, is well developed; aside from the Devinsky Commando, nobody has a sense of humor; and the texture of the book is attenuated, almost as if its social-realist worthiness might be compromised by too much verve and flair, like a wayward apparatchik in a flashy Italian suit.

CHAPTER TEN

Short Stories and Nonfiction

Barnes has never been a copious writer of short stories. Sometimes sections of his novels have appeared previously in periodicals: "Flaubert's Parrot," chapter 1 of the novel of that name, originally appeared in the *London Review of Books,* and "Emma Bovary's Eyes," another chapter, appeared first in a different form in *Granta.* It is not at all certain that, appearing without their novelistic context, they would have seemed to be fiction. A portion of *A History of the World in 10½ Chapters* appeared first in *The New Yorker;* but since it was the section of the book about Géricault's painting, readers could be forgiven if they failed to recognize it as a short story.

As for stories that are not parts of novels, there is a relatively slight fiction called "One of a Kind" in Malcolm Bradbury's *Penguin Book of Modern British Short Stories.*[1] It turns on two conceits: one is that Romania produces only one significant artist of each kind—one sculptor, one tennis player, one playwright, and so on. The narrator, talking this idea over with an expatriate Romanian, is led into a further discussion of a Romanian novelist (unlike the other examples, this one is a fictional creation) who wrote a "wedding cake novel," ironically modeled after the monstrous Stalinist architecture of Romania—an epic of vulgarity and excess designed to stand as an act of criticism of the reading public. Having promised to write just this book, entitled *The Wedding Cake,* he follows it up with several others, apparently popular. The ironies multiply, and the story concludes that this novelist, "Petrescu," is Romania's one ironist.

A few of Barnes's ideas about fiction surface in this story, which is largely an extended conversation between two writers; for instance, the Romanian exile, himself a novelist, explains his own troubles with the regime: "The few scraps of work I offered to publish were held to be insufficiently uplifting to the human spirit. Uplifting . . . ha. As if writing were a brassière and the human spirit were a pair of bosoms."[2] This remark is recycled: Geoffrey Braithwaite says "Do not imagine that Art is something which is designed to give gentle uplift and self-confidence. Art is not a *brassière*."[3]

In 1996 Barnes published *Cross Channel,* "a collection of short stories occasioned by historical meetings between the English and the French."[4] Four of these stories had appeared in periodicals: "Dragons" in *Granta;* and "Interference," "Experiment," and "Evermore" in *The New Yorker.*[5] Obviously the English-French cultural encounter is one of the central topics of Barnes's work, one which might easily describe the contents of *Metroland* and *Flaubert's Parrot* and large parts of *Before She Met Me* and *Talking It Over;* moreover, several short pieces that appear to be autobiographical essays about his own encounters with France could almost as easily be read as short stories devoted to this theme.

"Dragons," one of the strongest stories in *Cross Channel,* is historical fiction set in the wars of religion. It tells a plain story of a carpenter, Pierre Chaigne, whose family is destroyed and whose life is ruined because he is a Protestant (presumably; his faith is described only as "their cult," the persecutors assigned only to "the King's religion").[6] From the north come "dragons": these are soldiers, doing the work of the King's religion in persecuting heretics with the utmost ingenuity and cruelty. They are quartered in Pierre's home, ostensibly until he pays a religious tax; as they eat his food and burn his furniture along with the wood with which he makes his living, while redoubling the amount of tax owed, it is clear that the real aim is to convert the family to orthodoxy.

By means of mental cruelty, dishonesty, and sexual abuse of the thirteen-year-old daughter, they force the family, all but Pierre Chaigne, to abjure their faith. As the dragons leave the village, having converted all but eight of the heretics, Pierre prepares his dark lantern to venture into the forest again and practice his cult. The connection with England here is that the dragons, who speak a language unknown to the villagers, are actually Irishmen, wreaking their revenge on French Protestants for horrors inflicted on their country by Oliver Cromwell: though one of the dragons explains to Marthe, the daughter, that "You are heretics. Your heresy endangers the Holy Mother Church. All, everywhere, have a duty to defend Her,"[7] it is clear that hatred for English Protestantism is his real motive.

"Dragons" exhibits not only the interest in religion that has grown in importance in Barnes's work since the mid-1980s, but also his specific interest in heresy and religious deviation in France, which also figures in the chapter of *A History of the World in 10½ Chapters* called "The Wars of Religion."[8] Like that novel, this story is more concerned with religious history than with ritual or belief or sacrament; and the "balancing the scales" explanation for the Irish Catholic dragons' persecution of harmless French Protestants accords with the idea he expresses in that novel that history is just a version, the prevailing history being the version belonging to the victors.

"Interference" is about the artist, in this case an old English composer living in France. Leonard Verity is self-banished from England, considering his home country the enemy of art:

> He was an artist, did she not see? He was not an exile, since that implied a country to which he could, or would, return. Nor was he an immigrant, since that implied a desire to be accepted, to submit yourself to the land of adoption. But you did not leave one country, with its social forms and rules and pettinesses, in order to burden yourself with the parallel forms and rules and pettinesses of another country. No, he was an artist. He therefore lived alone with his art, in silence and in freedom.[9]

Technically he does not live alone, but with Adeline, his French mistress and lifelong companion, to whom this explanation has been given; the cruelty of telling her this is one sign of his great egoism. His residence in France is full of ironies: England, the enemy of his art, is where his music is recorded and performed, while in France nobody seems to know who he is; at the time of the story, he is anxiously awaiting a shipment of records from England so that he may hear his latest composition, called "Four English Seasons" (in which Adeline accuses him of "courting the country you deliberately left"[10]); he also is dependent on England, or the BBC, for broadcasts of music, though in order to hear them properly he must require that all electric motors in his French village be stilled to lessen interference with the signal. The climax of the story comes when he learns that his "Four English Seasons" is to be broadcast on the BBC; Adeline, who does not know this, fails to ask the villagers to shut off their electric motors, and the broadcast is spoiled, apparently resulting in Verity's death. This is a rich story, with penetrating observations about love and nationality as well as art.

"Experiment" is Barnes's finest short story. It is witty, oblique, and sophisticated. In many ways it recapitulates themes and motifs from the novels. Without postmodern play it raises the old question of truth and its verifiability.

The narrator is a doctor, apparently, who pays dutiful visits to an Uncle Freddy. Freddy often tells the same story, about his time with Surrealists in Paris in 1928. After a chance encounter with one of them (which one varies with the telling) in a bar, Freddy becomes involved in one of the series of Surrealist conversations about sex that came to be published under the title "Recherches sur la Sexualité, Janvier 1928–Aôut 1932."

This introduces the question of verification: since Freddy told this story for years to his dubious nephew and then died in 1986, while the "Recherches," including Freddy as the English guest "T.F.," were not published until 1990, the narrator is satisfied that the encounter really took place. The details vary from one telling to another, giving scope for witty puns in French. Freddy was in Paris on a business trip; asked by a stranger what his business was, or what he was drinking, he replied either "*Cire réaliste*" (wax polish), or "*Je suis, sire, rallyiste*" (navigator in a motor rally), or even "*Je suis sur*

Reuillys" (specifying his wine). Thus by linguistic mischance he is included among the Surrealists.

The story contains further revelations. One is that the Surrealists arranged an experiment to see if Freddy could tell the difference, sexually, between a Frenchwoman and an English-woman. He reports that "the French lass licked the raindrops from my face."[11] Still, finding the experiment creepy, Freddy leaves Paris at once on the boat train, where he meets Kate, whom he falls in love with and marries. This seems a stroke of wonderful luck.

The narrator, reading the "Recherches" after both Freddy and Kate have died, discovers that an Englishwoman, referred to as "K," was sometimes involved in the Surrealist experiments; and, reflecting after a wine tasting, he realizes (though this is only hinted) that the French and English women were the same woman.

The English in France; alternative versions of history; linguistic panache; the complications of sexuality, even among those who are said to be, like Kate, too innocent for the discussion of such matters—all are central Julian Barnes themes, here presented in a beautiful and terse fiction.

The reader remembers Geoffrey Braithwaite's discussion in *Flaubert's Parrot* of Emma Bovary's eye color, external and internal consistency and how these are related to truth. The narrator of "Experiment" thinks about the same questions, reflecting on the fact that Uncle Freddy always identified the car he was allegedly navigating in the French motor rally as a Panhard: "I used to divert myself by wondering whether such consistency on my uncle's part made this element of his story more likely to be true, or more likely to be false."[12]

Although, compared to many novelists, Barnes has written few works of short fiction, he maintains a high standard in this medium. His periodical work has consisted of diverse nonfiction much more than short fiction. He began his writing career as a freelance journalist. Though he has moved increasingly from reviewing toward personal essays and reporting, all three genres continue to occupy him. Despite his growing fame, most of his periodical work remains uncollected in book form, presumably because of his own misgivings about the wisdom of reprinting reviews and ephemeral journalism.[13]

He began as a reviewer of new fiction. Recently his reviews have seemed to concentrate more on nonfiction and on interests also manifested in his fiction: France, the intricacies of language, sexual mores. In a review of Eric Partridge's *A Dictionary of Slang and Unconventional English,* the former lexicographer shows a wide knowledge of slang, especially gay and cricket-related terms, and praises Martin Amis as a source of new slang.[14] Reviewing Francois Truffaut's correspondence, he has sharply interesting things to say about film and modern French culture, and shows a vivid metaphorical gift in such comments—on the comparative trendiness of two French directors—as "Truffaut was, as it were, just trying on the bell- bottoms; Godard was laying in a lifetime's supply."[15] His review of *The Perpetual Orgy,* Mario Vargas Llosa's tribute to Flaubert and Madame Bovary, sheds light on what it means to "love" Flaubert.[16] His early 1980s journalism also includes essays in newspapers about the *Oxford English Dictionary,* his former employer, and topics obviously relevant to his fiction such as obsessive jealousy and "obligatory sex" in a series on "the seven deadly virtues."[17]

SHORT STORIES AND NONFICTION

Personal essays, often autobiographical, have an interest of their own, as Barnes is both revealing and fairly modest, and generally writes with originality and verve. Noticeable, too, is a careful husbanding of resources, an ability to use the same autobiography more than once. For instance, a one- page essay called "My Hero: Julian Barnes on Jacques Brel," which appeared in 1989,[18] reappears in considerably expanded version four years later, entitled "1981";[19] in both cases the story is of Barnes's year teaching English language and culture at a Catholic school in France and his attachment to French singers such as Jacques Brel, Boris Vian, and Georges Brassens (whose death, in 1981, gives the later essay its title and its place in a book that has one essay or story for each of twenty-one years). "While English rockers strutted out their masculine domination, Brel sang of sexual hurt and romantic humiliation," he writes in 1989; in 1993 the rockers strut out "pit-bull masculinity," but otherwise the observation is unchanged.[20] The later, more extended essay provides much more detail on the singers but also much more about Julian Barnes's time in France and particularly the interesting topic of his relations, as an atheist, with the monks at the school.

"The Follies of Writer Worship" first appeared in *The New York Times Book Review* and was collected in *The Best American Essays 1986*. It starts with Somerset Maugham but circles around to a crucial event: Barnes's visit, during a French "studious pilgrimage" to authors' homes, to the Hôtel-Dieu in Rouen, where he saw a stuffed green parrot identified as the bird borrowed by Flaubert while writing "*Un Coeur Simple*"; two days later he saw the second parrot so identified.[21] Here is the germ of *Flaubert's Parrot*. What is striking here is that Julian

Barnes's reflections on the two parrots are much less full than those attributed to the less writerly Geoffrey Braithwaite in the novel: Barnes says

It was a droll, deflating moment, part Monty Python, part moral tale. The first parrot had made me feel in touch with the master. The second parrot mocked me with a satirical squawk. What makes you think you can seize hold of a writer that easily, it asked, and pecked me sharply on the wrist for my presumption.[22]

Despite the folly of writer worship, Barnes admits that he is in possession of a pack of cigarettes found alongside Arthur Koestler after his suicide. His fondness for Koestler and his feelings of inadequacy in his presence, along with the competitiveness which made him delight in beating the aged, ill Koestler at chess, are nicely recounted in "Playing Chess with Arthur Koestler."[23]

In recent years Barnes has done more nonfiction writing. Not only are his recent contributions longer, but they are less autobiographical and more authoritative. He functions more as a reporter, less as a memoirist, though the personal tone remains. The stimulus for this changed role seems to have been his recruitment in 1989 as *The New Yorker*'s London correspondent; he has explained the worries and attractions of the offer in his introduction to the collected *Letters from London:*

This could be a very nice job; this could be a life sentence; this could be well paid; this could be the novelist's classic trap. However, beyond these pleadings, I heard the most persuasive argument of all for taking the job: this will make you look. I-Spy London, here we come, I thought; I-Spy England.[24]

Letters from London 1990–1995 collects a powerful, intelligent, funny, and revealing five years of reporting on English affairs for American readers. The fifteen chapters are a mixture of political analysis, commentary on the arts, and contemporary history. Barnes, a Labour supporter, is wry and devastating on British politics in his five-year period. When he begins, Mrs. Thatcher is still leading the country (as parliamentary proceedings begin to be broadcast on television). He reports on her fall from the leadership; on the improbable rise of the colorless John Major; on the 1992 election, in which Barnes campaigned alongside Labour candidate Glenda Jackson in an election surprisingly won by the Conservatives; on the problems of the hapless and much-ridiculed chancellor of the Exchequer Norman Lamont; on Mrs. Thatcher's memoirs; and on the new Labour leader Tony Blair.

Barnes is a good political commentator, not just because he is well informed, with an original approach to his analysis, but also because of his style. His descriptions come alive. Mrs. Thatcher, during Prime Minister's Question Time,

> stands rather stiffly at the dispatch box, with swept-back hair, firm features, and an increasingly generous embonpoint thrusting at her tailored suit of Tory blue or emerald green; there, butting into the spray and storm of Her Majesty's

Loyal Opposition, she resembles the figurehead on the prow of some antique sailing ship, emblematic as much as decorative.[25]

He shows his linguistic and political acuity in criticizing Major for his desire to see wealth "cascading down the generations": "This seemed all wrong; in Mr. Major's world nothing does or should *cascade*. Waterfalls are much too dramatic: a metaphor from irrigation or, better still, plumbing would have seemed apter."[26] Geoffrey Howe, whose resignation speech began the process that led to Mrs. Thatcher's replacement, he characterizes this way: "Sir Geoffrey, like a one-sting bee that had done its business, now fell down behind the radiator, his distant buzz drowned by the whirr of an arriving hornet."[27] His ability to make characters, usually comic, out of such figures as Lamont and Howe is a tribute to his novelistic power. Howe and Major, who are best known for being colorless, are much more interesting and in some ways more alive in *Letters from London* than they are in life.

Relatively nonpolitical essays include one on garden mazes; one on fakery and forgery (based on an exhibition at the British Museum); one on the woman who modeled for the engraving of Britannia for a new issue of postage stamps; one on the enormous losses by investors in Lloyds of London; one on the Channel tunnel; and those on the Royals and the chess championship. Some of these skillfully weave together several topics: "Fake!" starts from the exhibition of forged paintings and moves smoothly and convincingly to the purchase of Harrod's by two Egyptian businessmen, who are suspected of having forged their autobiog-

SHORT STORIES AND NONFICTION

raphies and their statements of net worth, and the launch of a new daily newspaper, *The Independent.*

Though the prevailing tone of these pieces is urbane, ironic, knowing, often understated (describing one wacky American labyrinthologist as "leaning perhaps toward the intuitive in intellectual matters"[28]), he becomes most passionate in "Five Years of the Fatwa," about the death threat to Salman Rushdie, in which he writes movingly of the plight of Rushdie, defends free thought, and denounces various members of the British government and the British intelligentsia for their cowardice and moral fence-straddling.

Julian Barnes worried that he might fall into "the novelist's classic trap" in taking on the London correspondent's role. As he has published two novels and a collection of stories in the five years covered by *Letters from London,* there seems no sign that reporting has hampered his fiction writing. He has, meanwhile, disclosed an additional talent, for writing thoughtful commentary on contemporary life, which is both entertaining and informative.

CHAPTER ELEVEN

Conclusion

Writing in 1989, Richard Locke both pays tribute to Julian Barnes and offers his prediction of the books after *A History of the World in 10½ Chapters*:

> Barnes's literary energy and daring are nearly unparalleled among contemporary English novelists. With such a passion for history, art, and formal innovation, with such fulgent wit and bright discursive skill, he will most likely push on along the high Parnassian path he's beaten beside Nabokov, Calvino, and Kundera.[1]

This is high praise, and the novelists to whom he compares Barnes are heady company. One is struck by their internationalism—Nabokov the Russian-born cosmopolitan who lived in Germany, England, France, the United States, and Switzerland; Calvino the Italian postmodernist master fictionist and theorist; and Milan Kundera, the Czech fabulist, to whom Barnes had paid a tribute that implies kinship when, commenting on the tendency of some critics to deny his books the status of novels, he exclaimed, "Okay, let's throw out Rabelais, Diderot and Kundera. . . ."[2]

What places Julian Barnes at the head of contemporary English novelists? In addition to the qualities mentioned by Richard Locke—literary energy and daring—one must also recognize his ambitiousness. He aims high; none of his books is

CONCLUSION

an American-style "Big Novel"—crammed with data, nine hundred pages long—but each of his mainstream novels, at least, sets a high standard and achieves it. The ideas with which he engages are the important ideas—the relationship between art and life, the knowability of the universe, the meaning of history, the dimensions of bravery, the nature of love. He writes novels about world-historical matters, even if his usual characters are not world-historical people but rather people much more like his readers, that is, nonextraordinary without being uninteresting.

He is one of the most intelligent writers working in English, without giving the appearance of flaunting his intelligence. One aspect of this intelligence is his wit; another is his ability to use learning (about the ark, or about Bulgaria, or about France) without seeming to obtrude it or to force it in. There is almost never any feeling of forced learning included for its own sake. This is partly because, in almost everything he has done, there is irony and humor.

He is humane, and liberal in the "pre-post-modern" sense identified by Joyce Carol Oates.[3] Declaring that the truths of the human heart are the real center of his art would seem to ally him more with writers such as George Eliot and Nathaniel Hawthorne than with Kundera, Nabokov, and Calvino. Yet that is his focus: and in particular, as he has amply demonstrated, on love and its complications.

And Julian Barnes is distinguished for the cultural richness of his work. He is at home, intellectually and culturally, in France; he makes his readers feel at home there as well, as he does in the art history of a book like *A History of the World in 10½ Chapters*. Like his knowledge about biblical history or art restoration, his knowledge of high culture is lightly worn. Reading Julian Barnes, one feels that the novelist assumes a standard of cultural literacy that it is agreeable to possess.

Look again at the passage in which Richard Locke compares Barnes to Nabokov, Calvino, and Kundera. That in three years he would write a book that critics would compare to Orwell, Malraux, and Koestler was unimaginable at that point. But the capacity to surprise is one of his continuing strengths: the keynote to his career as a writer has always been versatility and change. Never content to repeat himself or to settle into a groove, he tries to make each book sui generis. He pays tribute to Flaubert's restless determination never to write the same book twice and believes that "In order to write"—surely this is unduly modest, and it should be altered to something like *in order to write greatly*—"you have to convince yourself that it's a new departure for you and not only a new departure for you but for the entire history of the novel."[4]

NOTES

Chapter 1: Career and Overview

1. Mira Stout, "Chameleon Novelist," *New York Times Magazine,* 22 November 1992, p. 29; Mark Lawson, "A Short History of Julian Barnes," *Independent Magazine,* 13 July 1991, pp. 34, 36.

2. The distinction between "mainstream" novels and "genre fiction," including detective novels, is certainly arbitrary and possibly unfair, but clear enough, and in this case Barnes's use of different names helps to reinforce the distinction.

3. Patrick McGrath, "Julian Barnes," *Bomb* 21 (Fall 1987): 22.

4. Stout, 72.

5. Kate Saunders, "From Flaubert's Parrot to Noah's Woodworm," (London) *Sunday Times,* 18 June 1989, p. G9.

6. Stout, 29.

7. Julian Barnes, *Letters from London* (New York: Vintage Books, 1995), 255; Stout, 72; Julian Barnes, "1981," in *21 Picador Authors Celebrate 21 Years of International Writing* (London: Pan, 1993), 93–110.

8. Amanda Smith, "Julian Barnes," *Publishers Weekly* 236 (3 November 1989): 73.

9. Ibid.

10. Ibid.

11. Julian Barnes, "To Suit the Occasion," *Times Literary Supplement,* 3 February 1984, pp. 113–14.

12. Andrew Billen, "Two Aspects of a Writer," *Observer,* 7 July 1991, p. 26.

13. Smith, 74.

14. Ibid.

15. Ibid.

16. David Sexton, "Still Parroting on About God," *Sunday Telegraph,* 11 June 1989, p. 42.

17. See Eric Metaxas, "That Post-Modernism," *Atlantic Monthly* 259 (January 1987): 36. In a comic article largely inspired by *Flaubert's Parrot,* he pretends to summarize recent novels, including *Flaubert's Panda,* by Boolean Jarnes, described as follows: "This one is part biography, part literary criticism, part fire hydrant, and part decayed wolf's pelt—in short, the post-modernist novel at its best."

18. Sexton, 42.

19. Lawson, 36.

20. Smith, 20.

21. Stout, 68.

22. Smith, 73.

23. Billen, 27; cf. Mira Stout's somewhat peculiar summary of his prose effects: "He observes a boring landscape and endows it with fanciful, wishful patterns and symbols—to pedantic and poignant effect" (69). Bailey 345; cf. Richard Locke, "Flood of Forms," *New Republic* 201 (4 December 1989): 40, who calls *Metroland* a "yuppie apologia."

24. David Coward, "The Rare Creature's Human Sounds," *Times Literary Supplement,* 5 October 1984, p. 1117.

25. McGrath, 21.

26. Mark I. Millington and Alison S. Sinclair, "The Honourable Cuckold: Models of Masculine Defence," *Comparative Literature Studies* 29 (1992): 1.

27. Millington and Sinclair, 7.

28. Ibid., 13.

29. Ibid., 3. Geoffrey Braithwaite does wonder if he is to blame: "At first I was hurt; at first I minded, I thought less of myself. My wife went to bed with other men: should I worry about that?" Julian Barnes, *Flaubert's Parrot* (New York: Alfred A. Knopf, 1985), 163.

30. McGrath, 23.

31. Coward, 1117.

Chapter 2: *Metroland*

1. Julian Barnes, *Metroland* (New York: St. Martin's Press, 1980), 33. Further references will be noted parenthetically in the text.

2. Paul Bailey, "Settling for Suburbia," *Times Literary Supplement,* 28 March 1980, p. 345.

3. David Leon Higdon points to the importance of Flaubert in Barnes's first three novels and comments on this one, "It comes as no surprise to learn that Chris's favourite book at this time is a pocket edition of Flaubert's *Dictionnaire des Idées Récues.*" See his "'Unconfessed Confessions': the Narrators of Graham Swift and Julian Barnes," in *The British and Irish Novel Since 1960,* edited by James Acheson (New York: St. Martin's Press, 1991), 176.

4. Ibid., 177.

5. See John Carey, *The Intellectuals and the Masses: Pride and Prejudice Among the Literary Intelligentsia, 1880–1939* (London: Faber & Faber, 1992). Chapter 3, "The Suburbs and The Clerks," is relevant to *Metroland.* Carey explains that to the twentieth-century literary intellectual, "'suburban' is distinctive in combining topographical with intellectual disdain. It relates human worth to habitat" (53).

6. Bailey, 345; cf. Richard Locke, "Flood of Forms," *New Republic* 201 (4 December 1989): 40, who calls *Metroland* a "yuppie apologia."

Chapter 3: Duffy

1. Richard Brown, "BARNES, Julian (Patrick)," in *Contemporary Novelists,* 5th edition, edited by Lesley Henderson (Chicago & London: St. James Press, 1991), 79–80.

2. A connection Barnes indicates by the allusion to Chandler's "mean streets" in *Fiddle City* (New York: Pantheon, 1986), 98: "He used

to stroll along Gerrard [in London's Chinatown] thinking: Down these chow mein streets a man must go." Future references will be noted parenthetically in the text.

3. Julian Barnes, *Duffy* (New York: Pantheon, 1986), 52. Future references will be noted parenthetically in the text.

4. Amanda Smith, "Julian Barnes," *Publishers Weekly* 236 (3 November 1989): 74.

5. Julian Barnes, *Putting the Boot In* (London: Jonathan Cape, 1985), 13. Future references will be noted parenthetically in the text.

6. Brown, 79.

7. Julian Barnes, *Going to the Dogs* (New York: Pantheon Books, 1987), 158. Future references will be noted parenthetically in the text.

8. Smith, 73.

Chapter 4: *Before She Met Me*

1. See Mira Stout, "Chameleon Novelist," *New York Times Magazine,* 22 November 1992, p. 68: "Barnes, Amis and McEwan wine, dine, holiday and play sports together"; see Martin Amis, "Snooker with Julian Barnes," in *Visiting Mrs. Nabokov and Other Excursions* (New York: Harmony Books, 1993), 154–58. Barnes's wife Pat Kavanagh was for a long time and until 1994 Amis's agent.

2. Amanda Smith, "Julian Barnes," *Publishers Weekly* 236 (3 November 1989): 74.

3. Julian Barnes, *Before She Met Me* (New York: McGraw-Hill, 1986), 17. Future references will be noted parenthetically in the text.

4. Mark I. Millington and Alison S. Sinclair, "The Honourable Cuckold: Models of Masculine Defence," *Comparative Literature Studies* 29 (1992): 13.

5. Though David Leon Higdon argues that Graham "virtually deserts his other responsibilities" in his obsession with Ann's "adul-

tery," in fact there is no suggestion that his behavior, no matter how bizarre, affects his job—possibly a commentary on the demands of a lecturer's position. See David Leon Higdon, "'Unconfessed Confessions': The Narrators of Graham Swift and Julian Barnes," in *The British and Irish Novel Since 1960,* edited by James Acheson (New York: St. Martin's Press, 1991), 178.

6. Julian Barnes, "Remembrance of Things Past," *Observer,* 24 July 1983, p. 22.

7. Patrick McGrath, "Julian Barnes," *Bomb* 21 (Fall 1987): 21.

Chapter 5: *Flaubert's Parrot*

1. Ann Hulbert, "The Meaning of Meaning," *New Republic* 196 (11 May 1987): 37.

2. James B. Scott calls it, with evident approval, "his 1984 novel, or rather, his trans-generic prose text." See Scott, "Parrot as Paradigms: Infinite Deferral of Meaning in 'Flaubert's Parrot,'" *Ariel: A Review of International English Literature* 21 (July 1990): 58.

3. This part of the book is taken from Barnes's own experience. See Julian Barnes, "The Follies of Writer Worship," in *The Best American Essays 1986* (New York: Ticknor & Fields, 1986), 1–8.

4. Julian Barnes, *Metroland* (New York: St. Martin's Press, 1980), 70.

5. Julian Barnes, *Flaubert's Parrot* (New York: Alfred A. Knopf, 1984), 166. Further references will be noted parenthetically in the text.

6. Terrence Rafferty, "Watching the Detectives," *Nation* 241 (6/ 13 July 1985): 22.

7. David Leon Higdon, "'Unconfessed Confessions': The Narrators of Graham Swift and Julian Barnes," in *The British and Irish Novel Since 1960,* edited by James Acheson (New York: St. Martin's Press, 1991), 181.

8. Higdon, 180.

9. Scott, 64–65.

10. The obvious literary ancestor of this technique is Laurence Sterne's *The Life and Adventures of Tristram Shandy* (1760–67), whose narrator regularly discusses the progress of his book and thinks of topics—for instance, noses—on which he needs to write a chapter, which he later duly does.

11. Julian Barnes, *Letters from London* (New York: Vintage Books, 1995), 290.

12. Andrew Billen, "Two Aspects of a Writer," *Observer,* 7 July 1991, p. 25.

13. Patrick McGrath, "Julian Barnes," *Bomb* 21 (Fall 1987): 22.

14. Higdon, 176.

15. McGrath, 22.

16. "Flood of Forms," *New Republic* 201 (4 December 1989): 41.

17. See Eric Metaxas, "That Post-Modernism," *Atlantic Monthly* 259 (January 1987): 36.

18. David Lodge, *The Modes of Modern Writing: Metaphor, Metonymy, and the Typology of Modern Literature* (London: Edward Arnold, 1977), 220–21. By "antimodernism" Lodge means to indicate the traditionalist, "common-sense" approach to fiction and poetry of English writers such as George Orwell, Kingsley Amis, John Wain, and Philip Larkin.

19. Lodge, 226.

20. Ibid., 229–39.

21. Barnes acknowledges in an interview (McGrath, 22) that some of this is aimed at "undercutting the academics."

22. John Bayley, *The Order of Battle at Trafalgar and Other Essays* (New York: Weidenfeld & Nicolson, 1987), 12.

23. Scott, 57.

24. David Lodge's Adam Appleby, pondering the same problem, decides that "Literature is mostly about having sex and not much about

having children. Life is the other way round." See *The British Museum is Falling Down* (New York: Holt, Rinehart, 1967), 63.

25. David Coward, "The Rare Creature's Human Sounds," *Times Literary Supplement,* 5 October 1984, p. 1117.

26. Rafferty, 22.

27. Smith, 74; Billen, 27.

28. McGrath, 22.

Chapter 6: *Staring at the Sun*

1. Andrew Billen, "Two Aspects of a Writer," *Observer* (7 July 1991): 27.

2. Carlos Fuentes, "The Enchanting Blue Yonder," *New York Times Book Review,* 12 April 1987, pp. 3, 43.

3. "A Short History of Julian Barnes," *Independent Magazine* (13 July 1991): 34.

4. Julian Barnes, *Staring at the Sun* (New York: Alfred A. Knopf, 1987), 68, 70. Further references will be noted parenthetically in the text.

5. Mira Stout, "Chameleon Novelist," *New York Times Magazine,* 22 November 1992, p. 29.

6. Amanda Smith, "Julian Barnes," *Publishers Weekly* 236 (3 November 1989): 74.

7. Ann Hulbert, "The Meaning of Meaning," *New Republic* 196 (11 May 1987): 38; Richard Eder, "Staring at the Sun," *Los Angeles Times Book Review,* 5 April 1987, p. 3; Christopher Lehmann-Haupt, "Books of the Times," *New York Times,* 30 March 1987, p. C16.

8. Stout, 70.

9. Charles McGrath, "Julian Barnes," *Bomb* 23 (Fall 1987): 23.

10. Julian Barnes, *Flaubert's Parrot* (New York: Alfred A. Knopf, 1985), 181.

11. McGrath, 21.

12. Kate Saunders, "From Flaubert's Parrot to Noah's Woodworm," (London) *Sunday Times,* 18 June 1989, p. G9.

13. Eder, 3.

14. See Billen (27), who reports that Barnes gave a friend the same gift.

15. Hulbert 39.

16. Mira Stout, when she sums up the book as taking Jean from childhood to death, seems to assume that she actually dies here.

17. McGrath 23.

18. Fuentes 3.

Chapter 7: *A History of the World in 10½ Chapters*

1. D. J. R. Bruckner, "Planned Parenthood and the Novel," *New York Times Book Review,* 12 April 1987, p. 3.

2. Mira Stout, "Chameleon Novelist," *New York Times Magazine,* 22 November 1992, p. 72.

3. Kate Saunders, "From Flaubert's Parrot to Noah's Woodworm," (London) *Sunday Times,* 18 June 1989, p. G9.

4. Robert Adams, "Balancing Act," *New York Review of Books,* 36 (26 October 1989): 7.

5. Richard Locke, "Flood of Forms," *New Republic* 201 (4 December 1989): 42.

6. Miranda Seymour, "All the World's a Fable," *Evening Standard,* 22 June 1989, p. 35.

7. Amanda Smith, "Julian Barnes," *Publishers Weekly* 236 (3 November 1989): 73.

8. Seymour, 35.

9. Jonathan Coe, "A Reader-Friendly Kind of God," *Guardian* (23 June 1989): 27; Joyce Carol Oates, "But Noah Was Not a Nice Man," *New York Times Book Review,* 1 October 1989, p. 13.

10. D. J. Taylor, "A Newfangled and Funny Romp," *Spectator* 262 (24 June 1989): 40.

11. David Sexton, "Still Parroting on About God," *Sunday Tele-graph,* 11 June 1989, p. 42.

12. Julian Barnes, *A History of the World in 10½ Chapters* (New York: Vintage Books, 1989), 109. Further references will be noted parenthetically in the text.

13. William Faulkner's *Go Down, Moses,* made up of fictions written at different times and published as short stories, is a novel, according to the author—and many other readers.

14. Locke, 42.

15. This Heaven is a bit like the afterlife imagined by Gregory in *Staring at the Sun:* "there might be a life everlasting so designed that you soon began to long for unattainable death..." (179). Here death *is* attainable, though it takes centuries before most people begin to long for it.

16. Gregory Salyer, "One Good Story Leads to Another: *Julian Barnes's A History of the World in 10½ Chapters, Journal of Literature & Theology* 5 (June 1991): 224.

17. Jonathan Coe raises an objection worth noting to this aspect of the book: "when there are such big themes at stake, the reader can get tired of being teased, however waggishly. It's like finally going to bed with the partner of your dreams and then, instead of making love, being given a jolly good tickle" 27.

18. Saunders, G9.

19. Julian Barnes, *Flaubert's Parrot* (New York: Vintage Books, 1984) 90.

20. Salyer, 223.

21. Salman Rushdie, *Imaginary Homelands: Essays and Criticism 1981–1991* (London: Granta Books, 1991), 241.

22. Richard Locke objects to what he calls "comforting intellectual clichés" and "nostalgic fluencies" (43).

23. Rushdie, 242.

24. Oates, 13.

Chapter 8: *Talking It Over*

1. Julian Barnes, *A History of the World in 10½ Chapters* (New York: Vintage Books, 1989), 238.

2. Julian Barnes, *Talking It Over* (New York: Alfred A. Knopf, 1991), 227. Subsequent references will be cited parenthetically in the text.

3. The married Gillian and Oliver move to the south of France, near Toulouse and the Canal du Midi, in the Aude. This is where Ann and Graham finally had their European vacation in *Before She Met Me,* having ruled out all the parts of the Continent associated with Ann's sexual past.

4. Bookworm [pseudonym], "The Flaubert's Parrot Sketch," *Private Eye* 772 (19 July 1991): 28. A review of Fay Weldon's *The Cloning of Joanna May* (1989) in the same magazine included this judgment: "Most of our novelists have become incapable of taking their own stories and characters seriously. Some brainy men, such as Julian Barnes and Martin Amis, have reacted by making their novels bags of tricks about how life is a bag of tricks." Francis Wheen, ed., *Lord Gnome's Literary Companion* (London: Verso, 1994), 166.

5. D. J. Taylor, "Fearful Symmetry," *New Statesman and Society* 4 (19 July 1991): 35.

6. Patrick McGrath, "Julian Barnes," *Bomb* 21 (Fall 1987): 21.

7. Julian Barnes, *Flaubert's Parrot* (New York: Alfred A. Knopf, 1985), 97.

8. A "turn-up for the book" is British slang for something astonishing, probably related to our "one for the books." Here, of course, it really means *for the book*—i.e., *Talking It Over.*

9. Christopher Hudson, "Three's a Crowd," *Evening Standard,* 11 July 1991, p. 36.

10. Anthony Quinn, "Money Can Buy Me Love," *Independent,* 20 July 1991, p. 26. See D. J. Taylor, *A Vain Conceit: British Fiction in the*

1980s (London: Bloomsbury, 1989): "English novelists have always been exercised by the problem of idiom: the solutions have been varied" (103). He goes on to praise Martin Amis for finding the most successful solutions.

11. This is colorful but, I conclude, wrong; Stuart reveals that Gillian had picked the faulty trolley and he was pushing it because she couldn't make it go straight. But his account is duller.

12. Zoe Heller, "The Square and the Other Two Sides," *Independent on Sunday,* 14 July 1991, p. 28.

13. Quinn, 26.

14. Julian Barnes, *Letters from London* (New York: Vintage Books, 1995), xiii. Oliver uses "inspissated" too.

15. This point is made in Taylor, "Fearful Symmetry," 35; Quinn, 26; James Wolcott, "Wizard Works on Vicious Triangle of Lovers," *Observer* (7 July 1991): 57; and (most strongly) James Buchan, "An Unsuccessful Likeness," *Spectator* 266 (20 July 1991): 25.

16. Taylor, "Fearful Symmetry," 35. In *A Vain Conceit* (70) Taylor wrote that the "great days of English experimental fiction belong to twenty or even twenty-five years ago."

17. Philip Howard, "Chattering Hearts in the Quagmire of Love," *Times* (London), 11 July 1991, p. 16.

18. McGrath, 21.

Chapter 9: *The Porcupine*

1. Paul Levy, "British Author, French Flair," *Wall Street Journal,* 11 December 1992, p. A10.

2. Robert Harris, "Full of Prickles," *Literary Review* 172 (November 1992): 26.

3. Julian Barnes, *Before She Met Me* (London: Cape, 1982), 74.

4. Julian Barnes, *Flaubert's Parrot* (New York: Alfred A. Knopf, 1985), 129–30.

5. William Leith, "Where Nothing Really Happens," *Independent on Sunday,* 2 May 1993, p. 13.

6. Ibid., 14.

7. John Bayley, "Time of Indifference," *New York Review of Books,* 39 (17 December 1992): 30. Comparisons with Koestler, particularly his *Darkness at Noon,* were noted elsewhere, for example, in Robert Stone, "The Cold Peace," *New York Times Book Review,* 13 December 1992, p. 3, and Josef Skvorecky, "In the Court of Memory," *Washington Post Book World,* 15 November 1992, p. 6.

8. Julian Barnes, "Stranger Than Fiction," *New Yorker* 68 (26 October 1992): 140.

9. Josef Skvorecky, who experienced Communist repression in Czechoslovakia, obviously found repugnant what he read as the suggestion that post-Communist societies are "simply the past in reverse" (6).

10. Julian Barnes, *The Porcupine* (New York: Alfred A. Knopf, 1992), 93. Further references will be noted parenthetically in the text.

11. Robert Harris (26) points out that the long list of decorations showered on Petkanov seems to be based on the West's embarrassing embrace of Romania's Ceausescu; but Petkanov is depicted as having been the most reliable ally of the U.S.S.R., while Ceausescu was perceived in the West, rightly or wrongly, as a rebel against Soviet policies.

12. Julian Barnes, *Duffy* (New York: Pantheon, 1986), 52.

13. Michiko Kakutani, "Confrontation Between Post-Soviet Bureaucrats," *New York Times,* 10 November 1992, p. C19.

14. Stone, 3.

15. The author addresses this matter in "Stranger Than Fiction" (140) where he relates how Bulgarian prosecutor Krasimir Zhekov, who had convicted real-life deposed Bulgarian strongman Zhivkov, approached Barnes and said, "I am Peter Solinsky."

Chapter 10: Short Stories and Nonfiction

1. Malcolm Bradbury, ed., *Penguin Book of Modern British Short Stories* (London: Penguin, 1987), 400–406.

2. Ibid., 405.

3. Julian Barnes, *Flaubert's Parrot* (New York: Alfred A. Knopf, 1984), 136.

4. *Granta* 47 (Spring 1994): 256.

5. Julian Barnes, "Dragons," *Granta* 32 (Spring 1990): 57–72; later reprinted in Giles Gordon and David Hughes, eds., *Best English Short Stories III* (New York: Norton, 1991), 16–30; Julian Barnes, "Interference," *New Yorker* 70 (19 September 1994): 94–100; Julian Barnes, "Experiment," *New Yorker* 71 (17 July 1995): 63–67; Julian Barnes, "Evermore," *New Yorker* 71 (13 November 1995): 104–12; Julian Barnes, *Cross Channel* (London: Cape, 1996).

6. Barnes, "Dragons," 60.

7. Ibid., 70.

8. See also Julian Barnes, "News from Elsewhere: On Revolutionary Kitsch and Compromise," *Independent Magazine* (29 July 1989): 16, about the history of the persecuted Cathar heresy in the Aude.

9. Barnes, "Interference," 95.

10. Ibid.

11. Barnes, "Experiment," 67.

12. Ibid., 64.

13. See Julian Barnes, "To Suit the Occasion," *Times Literary Supplement,* 3 February 1984, pp. 113–14, a review of Evelyn Waugh's periodical writings.

14. Julian Barnes, "Off-Street, Up a Gum-Tree," *Times Literary Supplement,* 3 August 1984, p. 860.

15. Julian Barnes, "Night for Day," *New York Review of Books,* 37 (11 October 1990): 14–16.

16. Julian Barnes, "Once in Love with Emma," *New York Times Book Review,* 21 December 1986, p. 10.

17. Julian Barnes, "The Social Democratic Phase," *New Statesman* 103 (16 July 1982): 20–21; Julian Barnes, "Remembrance of Things Past," *Observer* (24 July 1983): 22; Julian Barnes, "When It's Rude to Say No," *Observer* (20 June 1982): 27.

18. Julian Barnes, "My Hero: Julian Barnes on Jacques Brel," *Independent Magazine* 40 (10 June 1989): 46.

19. Julian Barnes, "1981," in *21 Picador Authors Celebrate 21 Years of International Fiction* (London: Pan, 1993), 92–110.

20. Barnes, "My Hero," 46; Barnes, "1981," 100.

21. Julian Barnes, "The Follies of Writer Worship," in *The Best American Essays 1986,* edited by Elizabeth Hardwick (New York: Ticknor & Fields, 1986), 2–3.

22. Barnes, "The Follies of Writer Worship," 3.

23. Julian Barnes, "Playing Chess with Arthur Koestler," in *Encounters,* edited by Kai Erikson (New Haven: Yale University Press, 1989), 23–34; originally published in *Yale Review.*

24. Julian Barnes, *Letters from London* (New York: Vintage Books, 1995), x.

25. Barnes, *Letters,* 11.

26. Ibid., 94.

27. Ibid., 51–52.

28. Ibid., 79.

Chapter 11: Conclusion

1. Richard Locke, "Flood of Forms," *New Republic* 201 (4 December 1989): 43.

2. Mark Lawson, "A Short History of Julian Barnes," *Independent Magazine* (13 July 1991): 36.

3. Joyce Carol Oates, "But Noah Was Not a Nice Man," *New York Times Book Review,* 1 October 1989, p. 13.

4. Andrew Billen, "Two Aspects of a Writer," *Observer* (7 July 1991): 27.

BIBLIOGRAPHY

Books Written by Julian Barnes

Metroland. London: Cape, 1980; New York: St. Martin's Press, 1981.

Duffy (under pseudonym Dan Kavanagh). London: Cape, 1980; New York: Pantheon, 1986.

Fiddle City (under pseudonym Dan Kavanagh). London: Cape, 1981; New York: Pantheon, 1986.

Before She Met Me. London: Cape, 1982; New York: McGraw-Hill, 1986.

Flaubert's Parrot. London: Cape, 1984; New York: Knopf, 1985.

Putting the Boot In (under pseudonym Dan Kavanagh). London: Cape, 1985.

Staring at the Sun. London: Cape, 1986; New York: Knopf, 1987.

Going to the Dogs (under pseudonym Dan Kavanagh). New York: Pantheon, 1987; London: Viking, 1987.

A History of the World in 10½ Chapters. New York: Knopf, 1989; London: Cape, 1989.

Talking It Over. New York: Knopf, 1991; London: Cape, 1991.

The Porcupine. New York: Knopf, 1992; London: Cape, 1992.

Letters from London. New York: Vintage Books, 1995; London: Picador, 1995.

Cross Channel. London: Cape, 1996.

Short Fiction and Journalism by Julian Barnes

"When It's Rude to Say No." *Observer* (20 June 1982): 27.

"The Social Democratic Phase." *New Statesman* 103 (16 July 1982): 20–21.

BIBLIOGRAPHY

"Remembrance of Things Past." *Observer* (24 July 1983): 22.

"To Suit the Occasion." *Times Literary Supplement,* 3 February 1984, pp. 113–14.

"Off-Street, Up a Gum-Tree." *Times Literary Supplement,* 3 August 1984, p. 860.

"Once in Love with Emma." *New York Times Book Review,* 21 December 1986, p. 10.

"The Follies of Writer Worship." In *The Best American Essays 1986,* edited by Elizabeth Hardwick, 1–18. New York: Ticknor & Fields, 1986.

"One of a Kind." In *Penguin Book of Modern British Short Stories,* edited by Malcolm Bradbury, 400–406. London: Penguin, 1987.

"My Hero: Julian Barnes on Jacques Brel." *Independent Magazine* 40 (10 June 1989): 46.

"News from Elsewhere: On Revolutionary Kitsch and Compromise." *Independent Magazine* 40 (29 July 1989): 16.

"Playing Chess with Arthur Koestler." In *Encounters,* edited by Kai Erikson, 23–34. New Haven: Yale University Press, 1989.

"Dragons." *Granta* 32 (Spring 1990): 57–72. Reprinted in *Best English Short Stories III,* edited by Giles Gordon and David Hughes, 16–30. New York: Norton, 1991.

"Night for Day." *New York Review of Books* 37 (11 October 1990): 14–16.

"Stranger Than Fiction." *New Yorker* 68 (26 October 1992): 140.

"1981." In *21 Picador Authors Celebrate 21 Years of International Fiction,* 92–110. London: Pan, 1993.

"Interference." *New Yorker* 70 (19 September 1994): 94–100.

"Experiment." *New Yorker* 71 (17 July 1995): 63–67.

"Evermore." *New Yorker* 71 (13 November 1995): 104–12.

BIBLIOGRAPHY

Articles, Sections of Books, and Reviews about Julian Barnes

Adams, Robert. "Balancing Act." *New York Review of Books* 36 (26 October 1989): 7. Review of *History.*

Amis, Martin. "Snooker with Julian Barnes." *In Visiting Mrs. Nabokov and Other Excursions,* 154–58. New York: Harmony Books, 1993. An account of the friendship, and rivalry, between these two contemporaries.

Bailey, Paul. "Settling for Suburbia." *Times Literary Supplement,* 28 March 1980, p. 345. Unsympathetic review of *Metroland.*

Bayley, John. *The Order of Battle at Trafalgar and Other Essays.* New York: Weidenfeld & Nicolson, 1987. Confident though apparently mistaken comments on *Flaubert's Parrot.*

———. "Time of Indifference." *New York Review of Books* 39 (17 December 1992): 30–32. Review of *Porcupine,* overemphasizing its political commitment.

Bookworm [pseudonym], "The Flaubert's Parrot Sketch." *Private Eye* 772 (19 July 1991): 28. Jeering review of *Talking It Over.*

Brown, Richard. "BARNES, Julian Patrick." In *Contemporary Novelists,* 5th edition, edited by Lesley Henderson, 78–80. Chicago & London: St. James Press, 1991. Literary encyclopedia article. Confident judgments on books up through *Talking It Over.*

Buchan, James. "An Unsuccessful Likeness." *Spectator* 266 (20 July 1991): 25–26. Harsh accusation that *Talking* is drawn from Martin Amis's *Success.*

Carey, John. *The Intellectuals and the Masses: Pride and Prejudice Among the Literary Intelligentsia, 1880–1939.* London: Faber & Faber, 1992. A brilliant account of the intellectuals' distrust and disgust toward the masses, including "suburbia."

Coe, Jonathan, "A Reader-Friendly Kind of God." *Guardian,* 23 June 1989, p. 27. Review of *History.*

BIBLIOGRAPHY

Coward, David. "The Rare Creature's Human Sounds." *Times Literary Supplement,* 5 October 1984, p. 1117. Thoughtful review of *Flaubert's Parrot.*

Eder, Richard. "Staring at the Sun." *Los Angeles Times Book Review,* 5 April 1987, pp. 3, 9. Intelligent review.

Fuentes, Carlos. "The Enchanting Blue Yonder." *New York Times Book Review,* 12 April 1987, pp. 3, 43. Very positive review of *Staring at the Sun.* Much treasured by Julian Barnes.

Harris, Robert. "Full of Prickles." *Literary Review* 172 (November 1992): 26. Review of *Porcupine.*

Heller, Zoe. "The Square and the Other Two Sides." *Independent on Sunday,* 14 July 1991, p. 28. Good review of *Talking.*

Higdon, David Leon. "'Unconfessed Confessions': the Narrators of Graham Swift and Julian Barnes." In *The British and Irish Novel Since 1960,* edited by James Acheson, 174–91. New York: St. Martin's Press, 1991. An analysis of narrators in Barnes's work. Useful.

Howard, Philip. "Chattering Hearts in the Quagmire of Love." *Times* (London) 11 July 1991, p. 16. Review of *Talking.*

Hudson, Christopher. "Three's a Crowd." *Evening Standard,* 11 July 1991, p. 36. Unsympathetic review of *Talking.*

Hulbert, Ann. "The Meaning of Meaning." *New Republic* 196 (11 May 1987): 37–39. Review of *Staring at the Sun,* with some commentary on Barnes's other books.

Kakutani, Michiko. "Britain's Writers Embrace the Offbeat." *New York Times,* 3 July 1990, pp. C11, C15. About Barnes along with Jeannette Winterson, Martin Amis, Peter Ackroyd, Ian McEwan, and others.
———. "Confrontation Between Post-Soviet Bureaucrats." *New York Times,* 10 November 1992, p. C19. Review of *Porcupine.*

Lehmann-Haupt, Christopher. "Books of the Times." *New York Times,* 30 March 1987, p. C16. Intelligent review of *Staring at the Sun.*

BIBLIOGRAPHY

Leith, William. "Where Nothing Really Happens." *Independent on Sunday,* 2 May 1993, pp. 13–14. Rumination on backwater status of Britain and its effect on writing, with some reference to Barnes.

Locke, Richard. "Flood of Forms." *New Republic* 201 (4 December 1989): 40–43. A review of *History,* but with some interesting looking back at Barnes's earlier works.

Lodge, David. *The Modes of Modern Writing: Metaphor, Metonymy, and the Typology of Modern Literature.* London: Edward Arnold, 1977. Contains some useful taxonomy of modern fictional stances and definitions of modernism, antimodernism, and postmodernism.

Metaxas, Eric. "That Post-Modernism." *Atlantic Monthly* 259 (January 1987): 36–37. A parody largely inspired by *Flaubert's Parrot.*

Millington, Mark I., and Alison S. Sinclair. "The Honourable Cuckold: Models of Masculine Defence." *Comparative Literature Studies* 29 (1992): 1–19. Historical survey of cuckoldry in literature, using *Before She Met Me* as one of the examples.

Oates, Joyce Carol. "But Noah Was Not a Nice Man." *New York Times Book Review,* 1 October 1989, pp. 12–13. Sympathetic review of *A History of the World in 10½ Chapters.*

Quinn, Anthony. "Money Can Buy Me Love." *Independent,* 20 July 1991, p. 26. Good on voices in *Talking.*

Rafferty, Terrence. "Watching the Detectives." *Nation* 241 (6/13 July 1985): 21–23. Strongly positive review of *Flaubert's Parrot.*

Rushdie, Salman. *Imaginary Homelands: Essays and Criticism 1981–1991.* London: Granta Books, 1991. Includes a wise review of *History.*

Salyer, Gregory. "One Good Story Leads to Another: *Julian Barnes's A History of the World in 10½ Chapters.*" *Journal of Literature & Theology* 5 (June 1991): 220–33. Interesting focus on theology rather than technique.

Scott, James B. "Parrot as Paradigms: Infinite Deferral of Meaning in 'Flaubert's Parrot.'" *Ariel: A Review of International English Litera-*

ture 21 (July 1990): 57–68. A thorough account of the poststructuralist reading of *Flaubert's Parrot.*

Sexton, David. "Still Parroting on About God." *Sunday Telegraph,* 11 June 1989, p. 42. A review of *History.*

Seymour, Miranda. "All the World's a Fable." *Evening Standard,* 22 June 1989, p. 35. Review of *History.*

Skvorecky, Josef. "In the Court of Memory." *Washington Post Book World,* 15 November 1992, p. 6. Negative review of *Porcupine,* castigating its political equivocations.

Stone, Robert. "The Cold Peace." *New York Times Book Review,* 13 December 1992, p. 3. Review of *Porcupine.*

Taylor, D. J. "Fearful Symmetry." *New Statesman and Society* 4 (19 July 1991): 35. Unsympathetic review of *Talking.*

———. "A Newfangled and Funny Romp." *Spectator* 262 (24 June 1989): 40.

———. *A Vain Conceit: British Fiction in the 1980s.* London: Bloomsbury, 1989. Sometimes insightful, sometimes wrongheaded survey of recent British writing.

Wolcott, James. "Wizard Works on Vicious Triangle of Lovers." *Observer* (7 July 1991): 57. Accuses Barnes of imitating Martin Amis.

Interviews and Profiles

Billen, Andrew. "Two Aspects of a Writer." *Observer* (7 July 1991): 25–27. Includes interesting quotations from Barnes and several of his friends; written in the style of the "Chronology" chapter of *Flaubert's Parrot.*

Bruckner, D. J. R. "Planned Parenthood and the Novel." *New York Times Book Review,* 12 April 1987, p. 3. Brief interview given at the time *Staring at the Sun* was published.

BIBLIOGRAPHY

Lawson, Mark. "A Short History of Julian Barnes." *Independent Magazine,* 13 July 1991, pp. 34–36. Brief but insightful.

Levy, Paul. "British Author, French Flair." *Wall Street Journal,* 11 December 1992, p. A10. Brief profile at time of *Porcupine*'s American publication.

McGrath, Patrick. "Julian Barnes." *Bomb* 21 (Fall 1987): 20–23. His most forthcoming interview. Here Barnes speaks frankly about his commitment to moral values in fiction.

Saunders, Kate. "From Flaubert's Parrot to Noah's Woodworm." (London) *Sunday Times,* 18 June 1989, p. G9. Includes some quotations from Barnes; a prepublication profile keyed to *History.*

Smith, Amanda. "Julian Barnes." *Publishers Weekly* 236 (3 November 1989): 73–74. Comments by Barnes at the time of *A History of the World in 10½ Chapters.*

Stout, Mira. "Chameleon Novelist." *New York Times Magazine,* 22 November 1992, pp. 29, 68–72, 80. A good interview of Barnes and overview of his work; the most revealing about his personal life.

INDEX

Adams, Robert, 108

Adultery, 13, 55–56, 58, 61–63, 64, 79–81, 94, 125. *See also* Infidelity.

Amis, Kingsley, 34

Amis, Martin, 3, 54–55, 142, 164

Bailey, Paul, 21

Barnes, Julian: and his life, 2–8; and journalism, 3–4, 52–53, 164–69;
    and comments on his own work, 4, 5, 6, 9, 10, 11, 13, 16, 42, 55, 68,
    90, 91, 93, 94, 108, 110, 120, 135, 147–48, 166–67, 169, 170, 172
    Works:
        Before She Met Me, 6, 7, 12–13, 45, 54–68, 70, 79, 80, 125, 144
        Cross Channel, 7, 159
        Duffy, 5, 6, 33–42, 43, 44, 48, 50, 55
        Fiddle City, 6, 35, 36, 42–45, 48, 50
        Flaubert's Parrot, 1, 6, 7, 8–9, 10, 11, 12, 13, 45, 66, 69–90, 91,
            93, 94, 95, 108, 110, 125, 135, 145, 147, 158, 159, 165
        Going to the Dogs, 6, 49–53
        History of the World in 10 1/2 Chapters, A, 7, 8, 9, 11, 69, 98, 108–
            124, 125, 135, 145, 158, 160, 171
        Letters From London, 4, 142, 166, 167–69
        Metroland, 2, 4, 5, 6, 18–32, 35, 54, 70, 79, 80, 91, 112, 125, 126,
            145, 159
        Porcupine, The, 7, 91, 145–57
        Putting the Boot In, 6, 36, 45–49, 50, 51
        Staring at the Sun, 6, 11, 12, 19, 69, 91–107, 108, 110, 112, 126
        Talking It Over, 7, 8, 19, 80, 91, 125–44

Baudelaire, Charles, 24, 31

Bayley, John, 86–87, 88, 149

Billen, Andrew, 77–78

INDEX

Booker Prize, 7–8
Bradbury, Malcolm, 158
Brel, Jacques, 165
Brown, Richard, 33–34, 49

Calvino, Italo, 171
Camus, Albert, 22, 99
Coe, Jonathan, 110
Coover, Robert, 110
Coward, David, 12
Cuckoldry, 13–15, 57–58, 79. *See also* Adultery, Infidelity

Deconstruction, 75–76
Doctorow, E. L., 111

Eder, Richard, 93, 100
Eliot, George, 16, 171
Eliot, T. S., 32, 106

Flaubert, Gustave, 1, 11, 12, 70–90, 93, 95, 108, 145, 164, 165, 172
France, 2, 3, 7, 18, 25, 30, 66, 77, 112, 126, 129, 130, 134, 159–63, 165, 171
French culture, 4, 6, 18, 21, 23, 25–26, 30–31, 55, 77, 80–81, 90, 159–63, 165. *See also* France
French language, 2, 82. *See also* France
Freud, Sigmund, 20
Fuentes, Carlos, 91, 93, 105

Hawthorne, Nathaniel, 171
Higdon, David Leon, 30, 74, 75, 78–79
Homodiegesis, 70–72, 113
Howard, Philip, 143

INDEX

Hudson, Christopher, 140
Hulbert, Ann, 93

Infidelity, 28–29, 54–55, 63–65, 79, 80–81, 125–27. *See also* Adultery

Joyce, James, 75

Kakutani, Michiko, 154
Kavanagh, Dan (Barnes pseudonym), 1, 5–6, 7, 36, 39, 42
Kavanagh, Pat, 7, 13
Koestler, Arthur, 149, 166, 171
Kundera, Milan, 9, 171

Lawson, Mark, 9, 91
Lehmann-Haupt, Christopher, 93
Leith, William, 147–48
Locke, Richard, 84, 109, 114, 170, 172
Lodge, David, 84–85

Malraux, André, 149, 172
McEwan, Ian, 54–55
McGrath, Patrick, 68
McInerny, Jay, 2
Millington, Mark I., 14–15, 57
Modernism, 9, 84–85, 90, 143. *See also* Postmodernism
Montherlant, Henry de, 22

Nabokov, Vladimir, 84, 171

Oates, Joyce Carol, 108–9, 110, 124, 171
Obsession, 12, 55–56, 59, 60, 61, 62, 64, 79, 96, 115
Orwell, George, 149, 171

INDEX

Politics, 4, 23, 28, 120, 145–47, 149, 157, 167–68
Postmodernism, 15, 84–85, 87–88, 120, 123, 124, 143, 171. *See also*
    Modernism
Pygge, Edward (Barnes pseudonym), 3

Rafferty, Terrence, 74, 90
Ricks, Christopher, 82–83
Rushdie, Salman, 4, 121, 123, 169

Salyer, Gregory, 118
Saunders, Kate, 97–98, 108
Scott, James B., 87–88
Seal, Basil (Barnes pseudonym), 3, 52
Sexton, David, 8
Sinclair, Alison S., 14–15, 57
Starkie, Enid, 81–83, 90
Stone, Robert, 157
Stout, Mira, 11, 93

Taylor, D. J., 110, 135, 142
Thomas, D. M., 75
Times Literary Supplement, 3 55

Vargas Llosa, Mario, 77, 164
Voltaire, 18

Woolf, Virginia, 33

Zamyatin, Yevgeny, 154